Preface

In the vast landscape of modern technology, understanding the fundamentals of computing is akin to possessing a master key that unlocks a world of possibilities. This book, dedicated to the exploration of computer fundamentals, serves as your gateway to comprehending the intricacies of these ubiquitous machines. Knowledge of computer fundamentals is not a mere luxury; it is an indispensable tool in the arsenal of modern life. Whether you're a seasoned professional seeking to deepen your understanding or a curious novice embarking on your first foray into the realm of computing, this book is tailored to meet your needs. As your companion in this voyage of discovery, we offer not just knowledge, but guidance. Whether you seek to bolster your technical prowess, embark on a career in technology, or simply satiate your intellectual curiosity, this book stands ready to accompany you every step of the way. Computers have revolutionised the way we live, work, and communicate. From smartphones and tablets to sophisticated data centres, the impact of computing is felt in virtually every aspect of modern society. A solid grasp of computer fundamentals not only empowers you to navigate this digital landscape with confidence but also opens doors to countless opportunities in various fields. In this book, we embark on a journey to explore the fundamental principles that underpin the world of computing. Starting with a historical overview of the evolution of computers, we delve into the essential components of computer hardware and software, covering topics such as data representation, operating systems, networking, logic gates and many more.

Now the question comes, **Who Should Read This Book?** The readership of a Computer Fundamental book extends beyond mere enthusiasts; it caters to a diverse array of individuals whose pursuits intersect with the realms of technology and information. Targeting a broad spectrum of learners, this tome is indispensable for aspiring technocrats, ambitious students, enterprising professionals, and curious minds alike. Students traversing the hallowed halls of academia find solace in its pages, as it encapsulates the requisite knowledge for mastering computer science fundamentals. Armed with this arsenal of understanding, they tackle assignments, ace examinations, and prepare themselves for the rigors of a burgeoning tech industry, where innovation and adaptability reign supreme. Seasoned professionals, entrenched in the trenches of corporate warfare, unearth in its depths a trove of wisdom to augment their skill set. From IT consultants grappling with complex infrastructure dilemmas to cybersecurity experts fortifying digital fortresses against insidious threats, this text serves as a beacon of enlightenment, illuminating pathways to professional growth and excellence.

Even those with a passing curiosity in the workings of technology find themselves drawn to its pages, captivated by its lucid explanations and insightful revelations. From retirees seeking to demystify the devices that now dominate daily life to entrepreneurs seeking to leverage technology for business success, this book offers something of value to all who dare to venture into its depths. In essence, the readership of this Computer Fundamental book transcends boundaries, encompassing a diverse multitude whose destinies intertwine with the digital zeitgeist. It is a testament to the ubiquity of technology and the boundless curiosity of the human spirit.

Best of luck in your preparations and your pursuit of excellence in the world of Computer Fundamentals!

Table Of Contents

Chapter 1: Introduction to Computers

In this chapter you will learn about:

Historical Development
Basic Concepts
Overview of Systems
Applications

Computers, ubiquitous in modern society, are powerful machines that have revolutionized the way we work, communicate, and live. At their core, computers are electronic devices capable of processing data to perform a wide range of tasks. From simple calculations to complex simulations, computers have become indispensable tools in virtually every aspect of our lives.

Understanding the fundamentals of computers is essential in today's digital age. Whether you're a student, professional, or enthusiast, knowledge of computers empowers you to leverage their capabilities effectively, solve problems efficiently, and innovate in an ever-changing technological landscape. With their potential limited only by our imagination, computers continue to shape the future of humanity in profound ways

1.1 Historical Development of Computers

The historical development of computers is a fascinating journey marked by remarkable innovations, visionary thinkers, and transformative breakthroughs that have shaped the modern world. From ancient abacuses to sophisticated supercomputers, the evolution of computing technology spans thousands of years, weaving together threads of mathematical theory, engineering ingenuity, and societal needs. This narrative unfolds through a series of key milestones, each contributing to the gradual realization of the computer as we know it today.

Ancient Origins:

The origins of computing can be traced back to ancient civilizations, where rudimentary devices were used for mathematical calculations and record-keeping. Among the earliest examples is the abacus, a simple counting tool consisting of beads on rods, which dates back to ancient Mesopotamia and Egypt. While primitive by modern standards, the abacus laid the foundation for later developments in computational devices.

Mechanical Calculators:

One of the most notable figures of this era was the German mathematician and inventor, Wilhelm Schickard, who designed the "Calculating Clock" in the 17th century. Although never built, Schickard's design featured a series of gears and dials capable of performing basic arithmetic operations.

Another prominent figure in the development of mechanical calculators was **Blaise Pascal**, a French mathematician, and philosopher. In 1642, Pascal invented the Pascaline, a mechanical device capable of performing addition and subtraction. The Pascaline used a series of gears and wheels to manipulate numbers, representing a significant advancement in computational technology.The 19th century saw further innovations in mechanical calculators, culminating in the invention of the Analytical Engine by the British mathematician and engineer, **Charles Babbage**. Conceived in the 1830s, the Analytical Engine was designed to perform complex calculations using punched cards for input and output. Although never completed during Babbage's lifetime, the Analytical Engine laid the theoretical groundwork for modern computers and is considered a precursor to the digital age.

The Birth of Digital Computing:

The true birth of digital computing occurred in the early 20th century with the invention of electronic computing devices. Among the pioneers of this era was Alan Turing, a British mathematician whose work laid the theoretical foundation for modern computing. In 1936, Turing published his seminal paper, "On Computable Numbers," in which he introduced the concept of a universal computing machine capable of performing any computable task. This theoretical construct, known as the Turing Machine, revolutionized the field of computer science and provided a blueprint for future electronic computers.

The Electronic Era:

The Electronic Era of computer history marks a transformative period characterized by the advent of electronic components and digital circuits. Beginning in the mid-20th century, pioneers like John von Neumann and Alan Turing laid the groundwork for electronic computing, leading to the development of the first electronic digital computers, such as ENIAC and UNIVAC. This era witnessed rapid advancements in semiconductor technology, culminating in the invention of the transistor, which revolutionized computing by enabling smaller, faster, and more reliable machines. The Electronic Era paved the way for the modern digital age, shaping the world we live in today with its unprecedented computational power and capabilities.

The Personal Computer Revolution:

The 1970s saw the emergence of the personal computer (PC), marking a new era of computing characterized by accessibility and affordability. In 1975, the Altair 8800, the first commercially successful microcomputer kit, was introduced by the American company MITS. Although primitive by today's standards, the Altair 8800 sparked a revolution in home computing and inspired a generation of hobbyists and entrepreneurs.

One of the most influential figures of this era was **Steve Jobs**, co-founder of Apple Inc. In 1976, Jobs and his partner, **Steve Wozniak**, introduced the Apple I, a pre-assembled personal computer designed for the mass market. The success of the Apple I laid the foundation for future innovations, including the Apple II, which became one of the most popular microcomputers of the 1980s.The IBM Personal Computer, introduced in 1981, further fueled the growth of the PC industry and established IBM as a dominant player in the market. The IBM PC's open architecture and compatibility with third-party software and peripherals set the standard for modern personal computers, paving the way for the widespread adoption of PCs in homes, businesses, and educational institutions.

The Internet Age:
The advent of the internet in the late 20th century revolutionized the way we communicate, collaborate, and access information. Developed by computer scientists and researchers in the 1960s and 1970s, the internet began as a project of the United States Department of Defense's Advanced Research Projects Agency (ARPA), known as ARPANET.In 1989, British computer scientist Tim Berners-Lee invented the World Wide Web, a system of interconnected hypertext documents accessed via the internet. Berners-Lee's creation democratized access to information and paved the way for the modern web, enabling users to browse, search, and share content from anywhere in the world.

The proliferation of the internet and the advent of cloud computing have transformed computing from a centralized, resource-intensive model to a distributed, on-demand paradigm. Today, billions of interconnected devices form the backbone of the internet of things (IoT), connecting people, machines, and data in real-time.

The Modern Computer:
Modern computer structure, function, and advancements represent a culmination of decades of innovation, resulting in sophisticated machines that power our digital world.The CPU acts as the brain of the computer, executing instructions and processing data, while memory provides fast-access storage for active programs and data. Input/output devices like keyboards, mice, and monitors facilitate interaction with the computer, enabling users to input commands and receive output.Advancements in computer architecture have led to remarkable improvements in performance, efficiency, and capabilities. From the development of multi-core processors and high-speed RAM to

the integration of solid-state drives (SSDs) and graphics processing units (GPUs), modern computers boast unparalleled speed and versatility.

1.2 Basic Concepts and Terminology

What is Computer ?

A computer is a sophisticated electronic device that processes input data according to a set of instructions to produce output. It consists of several key components, each playing a crucial role in its functionality.

Some Common Terminologies:

Hardware: The physical components of a computer system, such as the CPU, memory, storage devices, input/output devices, and peripherals.

Software: Programs and data that instruct the computer on what tasks to perform. Software can be divided into system software (e.g., operating systems) and application software (e.g., word processors, web browsers).

Operating System (OS): System software that manages computer hardware and provides services for application software. Examples include Windows, macOS, Linux, and iOS.

CPU (Central Processing Unit): The main component of a computer that executes instructions and performs calculations. It is often referred to as the "brain" of the computer.

Memory: Temporary storage used by the CPU to store data and instructions that are currently being processed. Common types include Random Access Memory (RAM) and cache memory.

Storage: Permanent storage used to store data and programs even when the computer is turned off. Examples include hard disk drives (HDDs), solid-state drives (SSDs), and optical discs.

Input Devices: Hardware devices that allow users to input data and commands into the computer, such as keyboards, mice, touchscreens, and microphones.

Output Devices: Hardware devices that display or present processed data to the user, such as monitors, printers, speakers, and projectors.

Peripheral Devices: Additional hardware components connected to the computer, such as graphics cards, network adapters, sound cards, and external storage devices.

Binary System: The number system used by computers, which consists of only two digits: 0 and 1. All data and instructions in a computer are represented using binary digits, called bits.

Algorithm: A step-by-step procedure or set of instructions for solving a problem or performing a specific task. Algorithms form the basis of computer programs.

These concepts and terminologies provide a foundational understanding of computer fundamentals, which is essential for further exploration and learning in the field of computing.

1.3 Overview of Computer Systems and Their Applications

1.3.1 Overview of Computer Systems:

Hardware Components: Computer systems consist of hardware components such as the Central Processing Unit (CPU), memory (RAM), storage devices (hard disk drives, solid-state drives), input devices (keyboard, mouse), output devices (monitor, printer), and peripheral devices (graphics cards, network adapters).The CPU executes instructions, memory stores data temporarily, and storage devices hold data permanently. Input devices allow user interaction, while output devices present processed information. Peripheral devices enhance functionality for specific tasks. Motherboards connect components, and power supply units provide electricity. Hardware components work together to process data, execute programs, and perform tasks in computer systems. Understanding hardware is crucial for building, maintaining, and optimizing computer systems.

Software : Computer systems run on software, which includes the operating system (e.g., Windows, macOS, Linux) that manages hardware resources and provides a user interface. Application software (e.g., word processors, web browsers, games) enables users to perform specific tasks.Software is coded using programming languages and executed by the computer's hardware. It encompasses a wide range of functionalities, from basic utilities to complex applications, and plays a crucial role in facilitating user interaction, data processing, and the operation of computer systems.

Data Representation: Computers represent data using binary digits (0s and 1s) called bits. Multiple bits form bytes, which are used to represent characters, numbers, and other types of data. Different data types are stored and processed using various data structures and algorithms.For example, integers, floating-point numbers, characters, and boolean values are represented differently in memory. Understanding data representation is essential for efficient data storage, manipulation, and communication in computer systems, enabling the processing of vast amounts of information in diverse applications.

Operating System: The operating system (OS) is a crucial component of computer systems, providing services such as process management, memory management, file system management, and device management. It serves as an intermediary between users and hardware, facilitating the execution of programs and managing system resources efficiently.It coordinates communication between hardware components and software applications, ensuring smooth operation and resource allocation. Operating systems enable multitasking, allowing multiple programs to run concurrently, and provide security features to protect against unauthorized access and malicious software. They are fundamental to the functionality of modern computer systems.

Networking: Computer systems can be connected to form networks, allowing for communication and data exchange between devices. Networking enables various applications such as internet browsing, email communication, file sharing, and online gaming.Understanding networking principles is essential for designing, configuring, and troubleshooting network infrastructures, ensuring reliable and secure connectivity in modern computing environments.

Security: Computer systems require security measures to protect against threats such as viruses, malware, hackers, and unauthorized access. Security practices involve regular updates, patches, and backups to mitigate risks. Furthermore, user education and awareness play a vital role in preventing security incidents. Robust computer security measures are essential to safeguard sensitive information, maintain user privacy, and ensure the reliable operation of computer systems in an increasingly interconnected digital world.

1.3.2 Applications of Computer Systems:

Business and Industry: Computer applications in business and industry streamline operations, enhance productivity, and drive innovation. They include enterprise resource planning (ERP) systems for integrated management of business processes, customer relationship management (CRM) software for managing customer interactions, and supply chain management (SCM) systems for optimizing logistics. Business intelligence (BI) tools analyze data to make informed decisions, while electronic commerce (e-commerce) platforms facilitate online transactions. Additionally, computer-aided design (CAD) software assists in product design, and manufacturing execution systems (MES) optimize production processes. These applications enable organizations to adapt to changing market demands, improve efficiency, and gain competitive advantages in today's dynamic business environment.

Education: In education, computer applications revolutionize learning by providing interactive platforms for instruction, collaboration, and access to vast educational resources. Learning management systems (LMS) facilitate online courses, assignments, and grading, while educational software offers simulations, tutorials, and multimedia content to engage students. Virtual classrooms enable remote learning and video conferencing for real-time interaction. Additionally, electronic textbooks and digital libraries offer convenient access to educational materials. Adaptive learning systems personalize instruction based on student progress, while educational games enhance engagement and retention. Computer applications in education empower educators and learners alike to explore, create, and excel in a digitally-enhanced learning environment.

Healthcare: In healthcare, computer applications play a vital role in improving patient care, streamlining administrative processes, and advancing medical research. Electronic health records (EHR) systems digitize patient information, enabling secure storage, retrieval, and sharing of medical data among healthcare providers. Medical imaging software assists in diagnosis and treatment planning by visualizing internal structures through techniques like MRI, CT, and X-ray. Telemedicine platforms enable remote consultations and monitoring, enhancing access to healthcare services. Clinical decision support systems (CDSS) provide evidence-based recommendations for healthcare professionals, while healthcare analytics analyze large datasets to identify trends and improve outcomes. Computer applications in healthcare contribute to better patient outcomes, efficiency, and innovation in the medical field.

Entertainment: Entertainment computer applications offer a diverse range of interactive experiences, from gaming to multimedia content consumption. Video games immerse players in virtual worlds, offering challenges, storytelling, and social interactions. Multimedia software enables the creation and editing of digital content such as videos, music, and graphics. Streaming platforms deliver on-demand access to movies, TV shows, and music, while social media networks provide platforms for sharing and discovering content. Virtual reality (VR) and augmented reality (AR) technologies offer immersive experiences in gaming, education, and exploration. Entertainment computer applications enrich leisure time, foster creativity, and connect people worldwide through shared experiences and digital content.

Communication: Communication computer applications facilitate seamless interaction and information exchange between individuals and groups across various platforms. Email services enable asynchronous communication through text-based messages, attachments, and organizational tools. Instant messaging platforms offer real-time text, voice, and video communication, enhancing collaboration and connectivity. Social media networks connect users globally, enabling sharing of thoughts, multimedia content, and social interactions. Video conferencing tools enable virtual meetings and collaboration among remote teams, reducing geographic barriers. Voice over Internet Protocol (VoIP) services provide cost-effective voice communication over the internet. Communication computer applications bridge distances, foster collaboration, and facilitate efficient exchange of ideas and information in today's interconnected world.

Scientific Research: In scientific research, computer applications empower researchers to collect, analyze, and interpret data more efficiently and accurately. Data analysis software enables processing and visualization of large datasets, uncovering patterns and insights that inform scientific discoveries. Simulation software facilitates virtual experiments and modeling of complex systems, allowing researchers to test hypotheses and predict outcomes. Bioinformatics tools analyze biological data, aiding in genomics, proteomics, and drug discovery. High-performance computing (HPC) systems provide computational power for simulations and data-intensive research. Scientific visualization software creates visual representations of scientific phenomena, aiding in data interpretation and communication. Computer applications revolutionize scientific research, accelerating discovery and innovation across disciplines.

Transportation and Logistics: In transportation and logistics, computer applications optimize operations, enhance efficiency, and improve supply chain management. Fleet management software tracks vehicles, monitors performance, and optimizes routes for transportation companies. Warehouse management systems (WMS) streamline inventory control, order fulfillment, and logistics operations within distribution centers. Transportation management systems (TMS) facilitate freight management, carrier selection, and shipment tracking for efficient transportation logistics. Global positioning system (GPS) technology enables real-time tracking of assets and vehicles, ensuring timely delivery and minimizing delays. Computer applications in transportation and logistics streamline processes, reduce costs, and enhance visibility throughout the supply chain, contributing to improved efficiency and customer satisfaction.

Personal Use: For personal use, computer applications provide a multitude of tools and entertainment options to enrich daily life. Productivity software such as word processors, spreadsheets, and presentation tools aid in work tasks and organization. Internet browsers offer access to a wealth of information, communication platforms, and online services. Multimedia software allows for creation and consumption of digital content like photos, videos, and music. Personal finance software assists in budgeting, tracking expenses, and managing investments. Gaming applications provide entertainment and relaxation through a variety of interactive experiences. Overall, computer applications for personal use enhance productivity, creativity, communication, and entertainment in everyday life.

The computer systems are versatile and pervasive tools with diverse applications across various domains, revolutionizing the way we work, learn, communicate, entertain, and conduct research. Understanding computer fundamentals is essential for leveraging the capabilities of modern computing technology and harnessing its potential to address real-world challenges and opportunities.

Summary

Computers: Integral to modern society, revolutionizing work, communication, and daily life.
Process data for tasks ranging from simple calculations to complex simulations.
Empowers individuals to utilize computers effectively across diverse fields.
Traces evolution from abacus to sophisticated electronic devices.
Introduces hardware components, software types, and operating systems.
Explores hardware-software interplay and roles of key components.
Examines computer usage in business, education, healthcare, entertainment, and more.
From early mechanical calculators to modern PCs.
Revolutionizes communication, collaboration, and access to information.
CPU, memory, storage, input/output devices, and advancements.
Manage hardware resources, provide user interfaces, and ensure system functionality.
Facilitates communication and data exchange between devices.
Measures to protect against threats like viruses, malware, and unauthorized access.
From scientific research and transportation logistics to personal productivity and entertainment.

Glossary

Evolution: Gradual development or change over time.

Milestones: Significant events or achievements marking progress.

Terminology: Specialized vocabulary or language used in a particular field.

Interplay: Interaction or reciprocal influence between elements.

Peripherals: Devices connected to a computer but not part of the core system.

Intricate: Complicated or detailed, often with small parts closely connected.

Diverse: Varied or different in kind.

Domain: Specific area or field of activity.

Streamline: Simplify or optimize a process for efficiency.

Implications: Consequences or effects resulting from a particular action or situation.

Previous Year Solved Question Paper

1. What are the different components of a computer ? Explain the role of each component with the help of a diagram. [IGNOU BCA 2023]

ANS: Central Processing Unit (CPU):

Role: Acts as the brain of the computer, performing calculations and executing instructions to run programs.

Components: Includes the Arithmetic Logic Unit (ALU) for computations and the Control Unit (CU) for directing operations.

Motherboard:

Role: The main circuit board that connects all components of the computer, allowing communication between the CPU, RAM, storage devices, and peripherals.

Components: Houses the CPU, memory slots, expansion slots, and connectors for peripherals.

Random Access Memory (RAM):

Role: Temporary storage for data and instructions that the CPU needs while performing tasks, enabling fast access and processing.

Characteristics: Volatile memory, meaning data is lost when the computer is turned off.

Storage Devices:

Role: Long-term storage of data and programs.

Types:

Hard Disk Drive (HDD): Magnetic storage, typically high capacity.

Solid State Drive (SSD): Flash memory storage, faster and more durable than HDDs.

Power Supply Unit (PSU):
Role: Converts electrical power from an outlet into usable power for the computer's internal components, ensuring stable operation.
Characteristics: Supplies power to the motherboard, CPU, and other components.

Graphics Processing Unit (GPU):
Role: Handles rendering of images, video, and animations for display on the monitor. Essential for gaming, video editing, and other graphics-intensive tasks.
Types: Integrated GPUs (built into the CPU) and dedicated GPUs (separate cards).

Input Devices:
Role: Allow users to interact with the computer.
Examples: Keyboard (for text input), mouse (for pointing and clicking), scanner (for digitizing documents).

Output Devices:
Role: Display or output data from the computer.
Examples: Monitor (displays visual output), printer (produces hard copies of documents), speakers (output sound).

Network Interface Card (NIC):
Role: Enables the computer to connect to a network and communicate with other devices.
Types: Wired (Ethernet) and wireless (Wi-Fi) connections.

Cooling System:
Role: Prevents overheating of the CPU, GPU, and other components by dissipating heat.
Types: Fans, heat sinks, and liquid cooling systems.

Previous Year Unsolved Question Paper

1. Discuss the working of central processing unit with the help of a diagram. Explain its various components. [IGNOU BCA 2023]
2. Draw the block diagram of computer. Explain function of each of the block.[Anna University BE/B.Tech 2011]

Exercise

Exercise 1 – Multiple Choice Questions

1. What represents the physical components of a computer system?

   a) Software
   b) Hardware
   c) CPU
   d) Operating System

2. What term refers to the programs and data that instruct the computer on what tasks to perform?

   a) Hardware
   b) Software
   c) CPU
   d) Memory

3. Which type of software manages computer hardware and provides services for application software?

   a) System software
   b) Application software
   c) Utility software
   d) Programming software

4. What is the main component of a computer that executes instructions and performs calculations?

   a) Memory
   b) Storage
   c) CPU
   d) Input device

5. What is the binary system used by computers composed of?

a) 0 and 2

b) 0 and 1

c) 1 and 2

d) 1 and 3

Exercise 2 – True/False

1. The IBM Personal Computer was introduced in 1981 and had a closed architecture.
2. Tim Berners-Lee invented the World Wide Web in 1989.
3. The internet began as a project of the United States Department of Defense's Advanced Research Projects Agency (ARPA).
4. Cloud computing has made computing more centralized and less distributed.
5. The CPU acts as the storage component of a computer.

Exercise 3 – Fill in the blanks

1. Computers are electronic devices that process _______ to perform a wide range of tasks.
2. The _________ represents the basic, yet significant, advancement in computational devices from ancient times.
3. Wilhelm Schickard is credited with designing the "Calculating Clock" in the ______ century.
4. Blaise Pascal invented the ________, a mechanical device capable of performing addition and subtraction, in 1642.
5. The ________ Engine, designed by Charles Babbage in the 1830s, used punched cards for input and output.

Exercise 4- Fill in the blanks with two options

1. Computers are essential tools in virtually every aspect of our lives, from simple ______ to complex ______.
2. The historical development of computers spans from ancient ______ like the abacus to modern sophisticated ______.
3. Wilhelm Schickard designed the "Calculating Clock" which featured gears and dials capable of performing basic ______ operations in the ______ century.
4. Blaise Pascal invented the Pascaline in 1642, which was capable of performing ______ and ______.

5. The Analytical Engine, designed by Charles ______, used punched cards for input and ______.

Exercise 5- Rearrange the sentence

1. "revolutionized powerful that work, the have computers are way machines communicate, we live and modern."
2. "the modern shaping world, have historical development by of computers innovations remarkable is the marked a journey."
3. "perform to a tasks of capable wide range are processing electronic data devices computers."
4. "rudimentary for used were devices civilizations ancient in calculations mathematical and record-keeping."
5. "Pascaline, addition subtraction the and performing capable of invented was Pascal Blaise."

Exercise 6- Choose the Odd One Out

1. CPU, GPU, RAM, HDD
2. macOS, Linux, ENIAC, iOS
3. Keyboard, Mouse, Monitor, Printer
4. Transistor, Resistor, Capacitor, Diode
5. Binary, Decimal, Hexadecimal, Algorithm

Exercise 7- Jumble words

1. UPC
2. SABCAU
3. OIRTANSTSR
4. UANTRI
5. UTIPN

Exercise 8- Match case

1. Monitor - a. Charles Babbage
2. Pascaline - b. Output
3. Analytical Engine - c. World Wide Web (WWW)
4. 1981 - d. Blaise Pascal
5. 1989 - e. IBM PC

Exercise 9- Assertion – Reason

Assertion: The invention of the transistor revolutionized computing technology.

Reason: Transistors allowed for the development of smaller, faster, and more reliable electronic devices.

Options:

A) Both Assertion and Reason are true, and Reason is the correct explanation for Assertion.

B) Both Assertion and Reason are true, but Reason is not the correct explanation for Assertion.

C) Assertion is true, but Reason is false.

D) Both Assertion and Reason are false.

Exercise 10- Read the questions given below and find the appropriate word in the grid provided.

A	L	M	O	K	N	R
B	C	N	I	L	O	A
M	P	D	N	N	D	M
O	U	T	P	U	T	O
L	P	G	U	I	L	F
P	C	O	T	J	L	B
K	B	M	K	F	S	M

Exercise 11- One- word

1. Tim Berners-Lee invented the World Wide Web in what year, revolutionizing access to information?
2. Computers use which number system that consists of only two digits: 0 and 1?
3. What term describes the main component of a computer that executes instructions and performs calculations, often referred to as the "brain" of the computer?
4. What type of memory is used by the CPU to store data and instructions that are currently being processed?

Hard disk drives and solid-state drives are examples of what type of computer component?

Exercise 12- Small Answers

1. What is the primary function of the CPU in a computer?
2. Who is credited with inventing the first mechanical calculator known as the Pascaline?
3. What significant development did Charles Babbage contribute to the field of computing?
4. What was the main purpose of the ARPANET project initiated by the U.S. Department of Defense?
5. How did the invention of the transistor impact the development of computers?

Exercise 13- Long Answers

1. Discuss the evolution of computer storage technologies from magnetic tapes and hard disk drives to solid-state drives and cloud storage. How has each technology impacted data accessibility and reliability?
2. How have advancements in microprocessor technology influenced the capabilities of modern computers? Compare the performance and applications of early microprocessors with those of today.

Answer

Exercise 1- 1) b , 2) b , 3) a , 4) c , 5) b
Exercise 2- 1) False , 2) True , 3) True , 4) False , 5) False
Exercise 3- 1) data , 2) abacus , 3) 17th , 4) Pascaline , 5) Analytical
Exercise 4- 1) (calculations, simulations) ,
2) (devices, supercomputers) ,
3) (arithmetic, 17th) ,
4) (addition, subtraction) ,
5) (Babbage, output)
Exercise 5- 1)Computers, powerful machines that have revolutionized the way we work, communicate, and live, are ubiquitous in modern society,
2)The historical development of computers is a fascinating journey marked by remarkable innovations that have shaped the modern world,
3)Computers are electronic devices capable of processing data to perform a wide range of tasks,
4)In ancient civilizations, rudimentary devices were used for mathematical calculations and record-keeping,
5)Blaise Pascal invented the Pascaline, a mechanical device capable of performing addition and subtraction.

Exercise 6- 1) HDD (All others are processing or memory units, HDD is storage.) ,
2) ENIAC (All others are operating systems, ENIAC is a computer model.) ,
3) Monitor (All others are input devices, Monitor is an output device.) ,
4) Transistor (All others are passive components, Transistor is an active component used in computing.) ,
5) Algorithm (All others are number systems, Algorithm is a process or set of rules.)

Exercise 7- 1) CPU , 2) ABACUS , 3) TRANSISTOR , 4) TURING , 5) INPUT

Exercise 8- 1. b , 2. d , 3. a, 4. e, 5.c

Exercise 9- 1) A

Exercise 10-

A	L	M	O	K	N	**R**
B	**C**	N	**I**	L	O	**A**
M	**P**	D	**N**	N	D	**M**
O	**U**	**T**	**P**	**U**	**T**	O
L	P	G	**U**	I	L	F
P	C	O	**T**	J	L	B
K	B	M	K	F	S	M

Exercise 11 1) 1989,
2) Binary System,

3) CPU (Central Processing Unit),
4) Random Access Memory (RAM),
5)Storage

Exercise 12-

1. The CPU (Central Processing Unit) executes instructions and processes data, functioning as the brain of the computer.
2. Blaise Pascal invented the Pascaline in 1642.
3. Charles Babbage designed the Analytical Engine, which was an early mechanical general-purpose computer that used punched cards for input and output.
4. ARPANET was developed to enable multiple computers to communicate on a single network, serving as a precursor to the modern Internet.
5. The transistor allowed for the creation of smaller, faster, and more reliable electronic devices, significantly advancing the field of digital computing.

Chapter-1
TEST PAPER
Introduction to Computers

Time Duration: 40 Minutes **Maximum Marks: 35**

General Instructions:

1. The question paper consists of 26 questions and is divided into four sections, A, B and C.
2. All questions are compulsory.
3. Section A comprises MCQs , Fill in the blanks and one word of one mark each.
4. Section B comprises question numbers 1 to 5. These are SQs carrying two marks each.
5. Section D comprises question numbers 1. These are LQs carrying five marks each.

SECTION-A

Fill in the blanks- **(1 X 10 = 10marks)**

1. Learning management systems (LMS) are commonly used in the _______ sector.
2. Electronic health records systems help in secure storage, retrieval, and sharing of medical _______ among healthcare providers.
3. _______ platforms deliver on-demand access to movies, TV shows, and music.
4. Email services are a form of _______ computer applications that enable text-based messages and attachments.
5. High-performance computing systems provide computational power necessary for data-intensive scientific _______.
6. _______ provides fast-access storage for active programs and data in modern computers.
7. Input devices such as keyboards and mice allow users to _______ data into the computer.
8. The _______ system manages computer hardware and provides services for application software.
9. The binary system consists of only two digits: 0 and _______.
10. An _______ is a step-by-step procedure for solving a problem or performing a specific task in computing.

True/False- **(1 X 5 = 5 marks)**

1. Binary system consists of digits 0, 1, 2, and 3.
2. Algorithms are step-by-step procedures for solving problems in computer science.
3. Computer systems consist only of hardware components.
4. The operating system manages computer hardware and provides services for application software.
5. Binary digits are represented by the numbers 0 and 2.

One word- **(1 X 5 = 5 marks)**

1. Monitors and printers are examples of what type of computer components?
2. What term describes the system software that manages computer hardware and provides services for application software?
3. What process involves coding software using programming languages which are then executed by the computer's hardware?
4. Operating systems provide what type of features to protect against unauthorized access and malicious software?
5. Which type of computer software includes word processors and web browsers?

SECTION-B

Short Question **(2 X 5 = 10 marks)**

1. What is the binary system and why is it used in computing?
2. Describe the role of an operating system in a computer.
3. What are SSDs and how do they differ from HDDs?
4. What was the significance of the Altair 8800 in the history of personal computers?
5. What does RAM stand for, and what is its purpose in a computer?

SECTION-C

Long Question- Write the 5 applications of computer. Explain them. **(5 marks)**

ANSWER

Fill in the blanks- 1. education, 2. data, 3. Streaming, 4. Communication, 5. Research, 6. Memory, 7. Input, 8. Operating, 9. 1 , 10. algorithm .
True/False- 1. False, 2. True, 3. False, 4. True, 5. False
One word- 1. Output Devices, 2. Operating System (OS), 3. Programming, 4. Security Features, 5. Application Software

Short Question- 1. The binary system uses only two digits, 0 and 1, to represent all data and instructions in a computer. It simplifies the design of electronic circuits and is fundamental to digital computing.

2. An operating system manages the computer's hardware resources, provides a user interface, and acts as a bridge between applications and the hardware.

3. SSDs (Solid State Drives) use flash memory to store data, providing faster access and greater reliability compared to HDDs (Hard Disk Drives), which use spinning disks.
4. Introduced in 1975 by MITS, the Altair 8800 is considered the first commercially successful microcomputer kit, sparking the personal computer revolution.
5. RAM stands for Random Access Memory. It provides short-term memory storage space for a computer where it stores data that is actively being used by the CPU.

MORE ONLINE SAMPLE TEST PAPER

Chapter 1 Test Paper – 1
Link: https://forms.office.com/r/VP76QY6N6G
QR Code:

Chapter 1 Test Paper – 2
Link: https://forms.office.com/r/AQT4KN7f0a
QR Code:

Online Resources

Online Exam Papers

MCQ Form
Link: https://forms.office.com/r/Ep3mk5by2E
QR Code:

True/False Form
Link: https://forms.office.com/r/E927ezgNc6
QR Code:

Fill in the blanks Form
Link: https://forms.office.com/r/TApyQEJ3CU
QR Code:

One word Form
Link: https://forms.office.com/r/AMnc9b6U9S
QR Code:

Rearrange the sentence Form
Link: https://forms.office.com/r/NZcmQkrYqP
QR Code:

Multiple Fill in the blanks Form
Link: https://forms.office.com/r/3f6qivnrvP
QR Code:

Choose the Odd One Out Form
Link: https://forms.office.com/r/XN1qTavqgQ
QR Code:

Jumble Words Form
Link: https://forms.office.com/r/n42bXA0EDZ
QR Code:

Match Case Form
Link: https://forms.office.com/r/Z9ZKFVyfGp
QR Code:

Assertion-Reason Form
Link: https://forms.office.com/r/q4vtgnuGV7
QR Code:

Videos

MCQ Video
Link: https://youtu.be/SIzJbcMrAzc
QR Code:

True/False Video

Link: https://youtu.be/5TQjPxR589M
QR Code:

Fill in the blanks Video
Link: https://youtu.be/Pf9tfKj9IdE
QR Code:

One word Video
Link: https://youtu.be/Wrh8m402kmA
QR Code:

Multiple Fill in the blanks Video
Link: https://youtu.be/u9TeY3XAbKc?si=slhP-gKaSojY-f32
QR Code:

Choose the Odd One Out Video
Link: https://youtu.be/hswwZWk9lbk?si=1tnOtsWhgb8WNWim
QR Code:

Short Questions Video
Link: https://youtu.be/WoZ7xmEscg4?si=DgipeqjkM8KQj2GJ
QR Code:

Long Questions Video
Link: https://youtu.be/vFZo56wdHrs?si=e0EFcvBg_LviYnKn
QR Code:

Chapter 2: Computer Hardware

In this chapter you will learn about:

Components of a Computer System
Types of Memory
Types of Computers
Storage Devices
Peripheral Devices

Computer hardware encompasses the physical components that make up a computer system. These tangible parts are essential for the processing, storage, and output of digital information, forming the backbone of any computing device. The primary elements include the central processing unit (CPU), memory (both RAM and ROM), and various input/output devices such as keyboards, monitors, and printers.

At the heart of these systems is the CPU, which is responsible for executing program instructions and managing the operations of other hardware components. Memory components, crucial for storing temporary data (RAM) and firmware (ROM), facilitate the smooth and efficient functioning of the CPU by providing quick access to data and instructions. Input devices allow users to interact with the computer, entering data and commands, while output devices display or produce results from the computer's processes.

Additionally, the field of computer hardware also delves into more specific devices such as storage units (hard drives and SSDs) and peripheral devices like scanners and webcams. These peripherals extend the functionality of computers, allowing for a broader range of operations, from digital communication to document digitization.

Understanding computer hardware is crucial not only for technology professionals but also for everyday users, helping them to effectively manage and troubleshoot their devices. As technology evolves, so too does hardware, with advancements leading to faster, more efficient, and more compact components. This dynamic landscape continually reshapes our interaction with technology, making a foundational knowledge of hardware an essential part of modern digital literacy.

2.1 Components of a Computer System

Central Processing Unit (CPU): The Central Processing Unit (CPU) is the primary component of a computer that performs most of the processing inside a computer. To understand the CPU, it's helpful to think of it as the "brain" of the computer, where most calculations take place. A CPU is made up of cores, with modern processors often having multiple cores. Each core can perform its own operations, which means that a multi-core CPU can handle multiple tasks simultaneously, enhancing the performance and speed of the computer systems. CPUs operate under the control of instructions from the computer's RAM, executing basic arithmetic, logical, control, and input/output (I/O) operations specified by the instructions. As an example, the Intel Core i9 processor is one of the advanced consumer CPUs on the market.

Modern CPUs incorporate technologies such as:
Hyper-Threading (Intel) or Simultaneous Multithreading (AMD): This technology allows each physical core of the CPU to handle two processing threads simultaneously, effectively doubling the number of tasks the CPU can perform at one time.
Integrated Graphics: Some CPUs have an integrated graphics processing unit (GPU), which can handle graphics and visual output without the need for a separate graphics card.
Thermal Design Power (TDP): This specification indicates the maximum amount of heat a CPU can produce under normal operation, which is crucial for managing cooling systems.

Memory: This component acts as the working space for the CPU, storing data and instructions needed in the short term. Primary memory includes Random Access Memory (RAM) and Read-Only Memory (ROM), which play crucial roles in the system's performance.
Input/Output Devices: Input devices like keyboards, mice, and webcams allow users to enter data into the computer. Output devices such as monitors and printers display or produce information from the computer, making the data accessible to users.

2.2 Types of Computers

The classification of computers into types such as mainframes, minicomputers, and microcomputers is based on their size, processing power, and intended usage. Each type has distinct characteristics and is suited for different purposes. Here, we'll explore these types in detail, providing a comprehensive overview and examples for each category.

2.2.1 Mainframe Computers

Mainframe computers are large, powerful systems used primarily by large organizations for critical applications, bulk data processing such as census, industry and consumer statistics, enterprise resource planning, and transaction processing.

Examples- IBM zSeries: IBM's zSeries mainframes are typical examples, widely used in financial sectors and by large corporations for massive data processing and transaction management.

2.2.2 Minicomputers (Midrange Computers)

Minicomputers are smaller than mainframes but more powerful than microcomputers. They are designed to serve multiple users simultaneously and are often used by small to medium-sized businesses for tasks such as database management, network management, and scientific computations.

Examples- IBM AS/400: Now rebranded as IBM System i, it remains popular in small to medium businesses and educational sectors for its robust application suite and reliability.

2.2.3 Microcomputers

Microcomputers, also known as personal computers, are the most common type of computer and are intended primarily for individual use. They range from desktops to laptops and tablets.

Examples- Tablets: Apple iPad and Microsoft Surface are widely used for their compact size and touch-screen capabilities, ideal for casual browsing, media consumption, and light productivity.

2.3 Peripheral Devices

2.3.1. Printer:

Functionality: Printers produce hard copies of digital documents and images, making them suitable for tasks such as document sharing, recordkeeping, and graphic design.

Types: Common printer types include inkjet, laser, dot matrix, and 3D printers, each with specific advantages and use cases.

Applications: Printers are used in homes, offices, manufacturing, healthcare, and various industries that require physical document output.

2.3.2 Scanner:

Functionality: Scanners capture physical documents, images, or objects and convert them into digital format. They are commonly used for digitizing photographs, documents, and artwork.

Types: Flatbed, sheetfed, and handheld scanners are available, each suited for specific scanning needs.
Applications: Scanners find use in offices, libraries, graphic design studios, and industries requiring document archiving.

2.3.3 Input Devices:

Input Devices: Input devices are peripherals that enable users to input data and commands into a computer system. They are crucial for tasks such as data entry, gaming, and controlling various applications. Let's delve into the most common types of input devices and their respective functionalities.

Keyboard

Functionality: The keyboard is one of the primary input devices used for typing text, entering commands, and performing various functions in software applications.
Types: Keyboards come in various layouts, including QWERTY, AZERTY, and Dvorak, and can be either wired or wireless.
Applications: Keyboards are used in virtually all computing environments, from personal computers to industrial control systems.

Mouse

Functionality: The mouse is a pointing device that allows users to move a cursor on the screen and interact with graphical user interfaces (GUIs).
Types: There are different types of mice, including optical, laser, and trackball mice, each with varying levels of precision and sensitivity.
Applications: Mice are widely used in desktop computing, graphic design, gaming, and more.

2.4 Types of Memory

Memory in computing is categorized into primary and secondary types, each serving distinct functions and having different characteristics. Understanding these can help optimize both the design and usage of computer systems.

2.4.1 Primary Memory- It is also known as main memory, is directly accessible by the CPU and is used to store data and programs that are currently in use. It is faster than secondary memory but is volatile (data is lost when the power is turned off) except for some types like ROM.
RAM (Random Access Memory): This is volatile memory used to store data and program instructions temporarily while a computer is running. It allows data to be read and written quickly in any order, hence the name "random access."
Example: DDR4 RAM in personal computers.
ROM (Read-Only Memory): Non-volatile memory that is used primarily to store firmware or bootstrap programs that initiate the startup process for computers.
Example: The BIOS found in personal computers.

2.4.2 Secondary Memory- Secondary memory refers to storage devices that are not directly accessible by the CPU and are used to store data persistently. This type of memory is non-volatile, retaining data even when the computer is turned off.
PROM (Programmable Read-Only Memory): A type of ROM that can be programmed once after manufacture. Once programmed, the data stored in PROM cannot be modified or erased.
Example: Microcontrollers used in appliances, which are programmed during manufacturing.
EPROM (Erasable Programmable Read-Only Memory): A type of ROM that can be erased and reprogrammed using ultraviolet light. This makes it reusable and flexible for tasks requiring frequent updating of the firmware.
Example: Early computer BIOS that needed to be updated without replacement.

2.5 Storage Devices

Storage devices are essential components of a computer system, used for saving data, applications, and operating systems. They vary in capacity, speed, form factor, and technology. Here, we explore various types of storage devices including Floppy Disks, CDs, DVDs, Hard Drives, and Pen Drives.

2.5.1 Floppy Disk- Once the standard for portable storage, floppy disks are magnetic storage media enclosed in a square case. They were primarily used for data transfer between computers and for backing up small amounts of data.
Example: The 3.5-inch floppy disk with a storage capacity of 1.44 MB.

2.5.2 CD (Compact Disc)- CDs are optical discs used to store data, music, and software. They have a storage capacity of about 700 MB. CDs are read by a laser and were a popular choice for music albums and software distributions.

Example: Audio CDs and CD-ROMs for software installation.

2.5.3 DVD (Digital Versatile Disc)- DVDs are similar to CDs but offer greater storage capacity and are used for storing videos, software, and large data files. A standard single-layer DVD can hold up to 4.7 GB of data.

Example: Movie DVDs and large software application DVDs.

2.5.4 Hard Drive- Hard drives are the primary storage devices in computers, used for storing operating system files, software, and user data. They can be either internal or external and use magnetic storage technology. Modern hard drives typically have capacities ranging from several hundred gigabytes to several terabytes.

Example: 3.5-inch SATA hard drives for desktop computers and 2.5-inch hard drives for laptops.

2.5.5 Pen Drive (USB Flash Drive)- Pen drives are compact, portable flash memory devices that connect via USB. They are used for transferring files between computers and as a quick backup solution. Storage capacities range from a few gigabytes to over a terabyte.

Example: USB 3.0 flash drives with capacities like 64 GB, 128 GB, or more.

Summary

Essential parts of a computer system include the CPU, primary memory (RAM and ROM), and various input/output devices such as keyboards, monitors, and printers, which collectively manage processing, storage, and data output.

Computers are classified into mainframes, minicomputers, and microcomputers based on size, power, and intended use. Mainframes handle large-scale processing, minicomputers support multiple users simultaneously, and microcomputers are designed for individual use.

Essential for enhancing computer functionality; includes printers for outputting documents, scanners for digitizing physical media, and various input devices like keyboards and mice for data entry and interaction.

Primary memory (RAM and ROM) directly interfaces with the CPU for quick data access and program execution. Secondary memory (PROM, EPROM) provides persistent storage for data that remains even when power is off.

Range from older technologies like floppy disks and CDs to modern hard drives and USB flash drives, providing a spectrum of storage solutions from portable to high-capacity needs.

The transition from mechanical storage like floppy disks to digital solutions such as SSDs and cloud storage illustrates the rapid evolution of technology, emphasizing the increasing efficiency and compactness of storage methods.

Glossary

Central Processing Unit (CPU): The primary component of a computer responsible for executing program instructions and managing the operations of other hardware components. CPUs can have multiple cores, allowing them to perform multiple tasks simultaneously.
Mainframe Computers: Large, powerful systems used primarily by large organizations for critical applications, capable of processing vast amounts of data.
Minicomputers: Mid-sized computers that are more powerful than microcomputers but smaller than mainframes, designed to serve multiple users simultaneously.
Microcomputers: Commonly known as personal computers, these are intended for individual use and include desktops, laptops, and tablets.
Pen Drive (USB Flash Drive): A portable storage device that connects via USB, used for transferring files between computers and as a quick backup solution.
Simultaneous Multithreading: A technology that allows each physical core of the CPU to handle two processing threads at once, effectively doubling the tasks the CPU can perform simultaneously.
Thermal Design Power (TDP): The maximum amount of heat a CPU or any computer component can generate under normal operation, which is critical for managing cooling systems.

Previous Year Solved Question Paper

1. Differentiate between the CD-ROM and Hard disk [IGNOU BCA 2023]
ANS: CD-ROM (Compact Disc Read-Only Memory):
Storage Capacity: Typically up to 700 MB.
Data Access: Slower access speeds compared to hard disks.
Durability: More prone to scratches and physical damage.
Usage: Commonly used for distributing software, music, and multimedia.
Reusability: Read-only; cannot be written or erased (except CD-RW variants).
Portability: Highly portable due to its small, lightweight nature.
Construction: Optical disc using laser technology to read data.
Hard Disk:
Storage Capacity: Ranges from several GB to multiple TB (terabytes).
Data Access: Faster access speeds and higher data transfer rates.

Durability: Generally more robust, but can be damaged by physical shocks.

Usage: Used for storing operating systems, software, and large amounts of data.

Reusability: Can be written and rewritten multiple times.

Portability: Less portable, especially internal hard disks; external hard disks offer some portability.

Construction: Magnetic disk with read/write heads for accessing data.

Previous Year Unsolved Question Paper

1. Compare Primary and Secondary Memories. Discuss various types of main memories. [IGNOU BCA 2023]
2. Define main memory. How the different types of memory are classified? Discuss with neat diagram[Anna University BE/B.Tech 2011]

Exercise

Exercise 1 – Multiple Choice Questions

1. What is the primary function of the CPU in a computer system?
A) Data storage
B) Execute program instructions
C) Power supply
D) External communication

2. Which type of memory is volatile?
A) RAM
B) ROM
C) EPROM
D) PROM

3. What is the purpose of input devices for a computer?
A) To display data
B) To enter data into the computer
C) To store data
D) To cool the computer

4. Which device is used to make hard copies of digital documents?

A) Scanner
B) Monitor
C) Printer
D) Keyboard

5. What does 'Hyper-Threading' technology in CPUs allow?
A) Increase storage capacity
B) Enhance audio output
C) Each core to handle multiple threads
D) Reduce power consumption

Exercise 2 – True/False

1. The CPU performs most of the calculations in a computer.
2. ROM is a volatile type of memory.
3. A scanner is an output device.
4. Hyper-Threading technology is used in AMD processors.
5. Mainframe computers are primarily designed for individual use.

Exercise 3 – Fill in the blanks

1. The CPU is often referred to as the ______ of the computer.
2. ______ memory loses its data when power is turned off.
3. A ______ uses a laser to read and write data.
4. Mainframe computers are used for ______ processing.
5. A ______ is used to enter data into a computer.

Exercise 4- Fill in the blanks with two options

1. A ______ can store data temporarily, while a ______ is used for long-term data storage.
2. ______ are used for data input, whereas ______ are used for data output in a computer system.
3. A ______ uses optical technology for data reading, while a ______ uses magnetic technology.
4. ______ memory is volatile and temporary, whereas ______ memory retains data even when powered off.
5. The function of a ______ is to enter commands, and a ______ displays the results.

Exercise 5- Small Answers

1. What is the main function of the CPU in a computer?
2. What type of memory is RAM and what is its function?
3. Name two types of input devices.
4. What is the primary use of a scanner?
5. What technology allows a CPU core to handle two processing threads simultaneously?

Exercise 6- Long Answers

1. Explain how a CPU is similar to the brain of a computer.
2. Discuss the evolution of storage devices from floppy disks to SSDs.

Answer

Exercise 1- 1) b , 2) a , 3) b , 4) c , 5) c
Exercise 2- 1) True , 2) False , 3) False , 4) False , 5) False
Exercise 3- 1) brain , 2) Volatile , 3) CD , 4) large-scale , 5) keyboard
Exercise 4- 1) RAM, hard drive,
2) Keyboards, monitors ,
3) CD, hard drive ,
4) RAM, ROM ,
5) keyboard, monitor

Exercise 5-

1. The CPU executes program instructions and manages the operations of other hardware components in a computer.
2. RAM is volatile memory used to store data and program instructions temporarily, facilitating quick access for the CPU.
3. Keyboard and mouse.
4. A scanner captures physical documents and images and converts them into digital format.
5. Hyper-Threading (Intel) or Simultaneous Multithreading (AMD).

Chapter-2
TEST PAPER
Introduction to Computers

Time Duration: 30 Minutes **Maximum Marks: 25**

General Instructions:

1. The question paper consists of 26 questions and is divided into four sections, A, B and C.
2. All questions are compulsory.
3. Section A comprises MCQs, Fill in the blanks and one word of one mark each.
4. Section B comprises question numbers 1 to 5. These are SQs carrying two marks each.
5. Section D comprises question numbers 1. These are LQs, each carrying five marks.

SECTION-A

Fill in the blanks- **(1 X 5 = 5 marks)**

1. The main function of _______ is to store programs and data currently being used by the CPU.
2. A _______ is typically used in enterprise environments where large-scale processing and data storage is required.
3. Data stored in _______ memory can be accessed directly by the CPU without any intermediary system.
4. The _______ mouse uses a light-emitting diode and photodiodes to detect movement relative to the underlying surface.
5. The primary function of the _______ is to execute program instructions and manage system resources.

MCQ- **(1 X 5 = 5 marks)**

1. Which component is essential for a computer to perform basic arithmetic, logical, control, and input/output operations?
   A) Hard Drive
   B) RAM
   C) CPU
   D) GPU
2. Which memory type is used primarily during the startup process of a computer?
   A) SSD
   B) DDR4 RAM
   C) ROM
   D) USB Flash Drive
3. What does a scanner typically digitize?
   A) Digital images only
   B) Documents and photographs
   C) Audio files
   D) Video clips
4. Which technology would be used in a CPU to manage cooling systems based on heat production?
   A) Multi-Core Processing
   B) Integrated Graphics
   C) Thermal Design Power (TDP)
   D) Hyper-Threading
5. What type of computer is often used by individuals for personal tasks such as browsing the web and using office applications?
   A) Mainframe
   B) Microcomputer
   C) Minicomputer
   D) Supercomputer

SECTION-B

Short Question- **(2 X 5 = 10 marks)**

1. What is the role of a printer in a computer system?
2. Describe the function of ROM in a computer system.
3. What are the advantages of using SSDs over traditional hard drives?
4. Why is RAM considered volatile?
5. Explain the function of a webcam in a computer system.

SECTION-C

Long Question- . **(5 X 1 = 5 marks)**

1. Discuss the various types of computer memory and their importance in the functioning of a computer system.

ONLINE RESOURCES

Chapter 2 Practice Paper
Link: https://forms.gle/zonmHfYwEpiq6ZBT8
QR Code:

Chapter 2 Video Content
Link: https://youtu.be/oBR_54gO-uc?si=Y4fp_sB1TjgmdvAB
QR Code:

Chapter 3: Computer Software

In this chapter you will learn about:

Types of Software
Operating Systems and Utility Programs
Overview of Programming Languages

3.1 Types of Software

In the realm of computing, software can be broadly categorized into two main types: System Software and Application Software. Each type serves distinct purposes, catering to various operational needs of a computer system.System software and application software are integral to the functionality of modern computers, each fulfilling crucial roles. System software provides the necessary platform and tools to run hardware and manage resources efficiently, while application software directly assists users in performing specific, task-oriented functions. Together, they enable diverse computing experiences, catering to various personal and professional needs.

3.1.1 System Software

System software serves as the fundamental interface between hardware and user applications. It is designed to manage the system resources and provide a platform for running application software.

Operating Systems: The core software that manages hardware resources, provides common services for computer programs, and allows for user interaction with the hardware. Examples include Windows, macOS, and Linux.

Device Drivers: These are specific types of system software that allow higher-level computer programs to interact with a hardware device. Examples include printer drivers, display drivers, and USB drivers.

Utility Programs: Software designed to help manage, maintain, and control computer resources. Examples include antivirus programs, file management tools, and backup software.

3.1.2 Application Software

Application software is designed to perform specific tasks for users. These tasks can range from productivity and data management to entertainment and design.

Productivity Software: Tools that help users produce things like documents, databases, graphs, and presentations. Examples include Microsoft Office, Google Workspace, and Adobe Acrobat.
Database Software: Systems that allow users to store, modify, and extract information from a database. Examples include Oracle, MySQL, and Microsoft SQL Server.
Media Software: Programs designed for creating and editing graphics, video, and music. Examples include Adobe Photoshop, Final Cut Pro, and Ableton Live.
Web Browsers: Software used to browse the internet. Examples include Google Chrome, Mozilla Firefox, and Safari.
Educational Software: Applications designed specifically for learning purposes. Examples include Duolingo for language learning and Khan Academy for a wide range of educational content.

3.2 Operating Systems and Utility Programs

Operating systems and utility programs are foundational components of computer functionality, each playing a crucial role in the management and efficiency of computing resources.Operating systems and utility programs are integral to the operational efficacy and security of computer systems. While operating systems provide the necessary groundwork and resources for all computing activities, utility programs enhance and optimize these operations, ensuring that the system remains efficient, secure, and well-maintained. Together, they form the backbone of a computer's functionality, enabling both basic and advanced computing tasks.

3.2.1 Operating Systems (OS)

An operating system is the core software that manages computer hardware, software resources, and provides common services for computer programs. It acts as an intermediary between users and the computer hardware.

Resource Management: Manages the hardware resources of the computer such as CPU, memory, disk space, and peripheral devices.
Task Scheduling: Efficiently manages the execution of multiple tasks, often giving the illusion of concurrency on processors with a single core.
User Interface: Provides a graphical user interface (GUI) or command-line interface (CLI) for users to interact with the system.
Examples- Windows, macOS, Linux .

3.2.2 Utility Programs

Utility programs are software designed to help analyze, configure, optimize, or maintain a computer. They are often viewed as a subset of system software, directly interacting with the operating system to perform specific tasks.

System Maintenance: Tools that help in cleaning up unnecessary files, defragmenting disks, scanning for malware, and backing up data.
System Monitoring: Utilities that monitor system resources and performance, such as CPU usage, memory usage, and network traffic.
File Management: Tools designed to manage files and directories, providing functions beyond those available in the operating system.
Examples- Antivirus Software, Disk Cleaner, Backup Software, File Compression Tools .

3.3 Overview of Programming Languages: Machine, Assembly, and High-Level Languages

Programming languages are the fundamental tools used to instruct computers and are categorized based on their level of abstraction and closeness to human language. These categories include machine language, assembly language, and high-level languages, each serving different purposes and offering different benefits.The spectrum of programming languages from machine to high-level languages represents a transition from a focus on direct hardware manipulation to emphasizing problem-solving and application development. Each category serves its purpose, from performing hardware-level operations in machine and assembly languages to developing complex, portable applications in high-level languages. This hierarchy not only aids in educational understanding but also in practical applications, catering to the needs of different programming environments and challenges.

3.3.1 Machine Language

Machine language is the lowest level of programming language, consisting of binary code that is directly understood by a computer's CPU. It is specific to the architecture of the computer's processor and is the most basic form of instruction a computer can execute.
Binary Code: Composed entirely of 0s and 1s, which represent on/off signals that the processor can interpret.
Processor-Specific: Each type of processor has its own unique machine language.
Example- Direct binary commands entered into a micro controller or a primitive computer system.

3.3.2 Assembly Language

Assembly language is one step above machine language and uses mnemonic codes or symbols instead of binary to represent operations. It is still closely tied to the architecture of the CPU but is more readable than machine language.

Low-level: Although more abstract than machine language, assembly is still considered low-level and requires a thorough understanding of the computer's architecture.

Assembler: Requires a tool called an assembler to convert the assembly code into machine code that the computer can execute.

Example- Using Assembly for programming embedded systems, where precise control over hardware is required, such as in robotics or real-time system processing.

3.3.3 High-Level Languages

High-level programming languages are closer to human languages and far removed from the hardware details. They are designed to be easy to read and write, with a syntax that expresses more complex operations in a single statement.

Abstraction: High-level languages abstract the details of the computer hardware, allowing the programmer to focus on the logic of the program without worrying about the specifics of the underlying hardware.

Portability: Codes written in high-level languages can often be run on multiple platforms without modification.

Examples- Python, Java, C++ .

SUMMARY

Software is divided into system software, which facilitates the operation of hardware and system resources, and application software, designed for user-oriented tasks.

Includes operating systems like Windows, macOS, and Linux, which manage hardware resources, and utility programs that optimize and maintain system performance.

Encompasses productivity tools like Microsoft Office, database systems such as MySQL, media software such as Adobe Photoshop, web browsers like Chrome, and educational software like Khan Academy.

Essential for resource management, task scheduling, and user interaction, providing both GUI and CLI interfaces.

Include antivirus software, disk cleaners, and backup tools, enhancing system maintenance, monitoring, and file management.

Categorized by abstraction level from machine languages (low-level, directly executed by CPU) to high-level languages (abstract, portable, user-friendly), facilitating a range of tasks from hardware control to application development.

GLOSSARY

System Software: Software that manages hardware resources and provides a platform for running application software.
Application Software: Software designed to perform specific user-oriented tasks, such as productivity or entertainment.
Operating Systems (OS): The core system software that manages computer hardware, software resources, and provides common services for computer programs.
Device Drivers: Software that allows higher-level computer programs to interact with a hardware device.
Utility Programs: Software designed to help manage, maintain, and control computer resources.
Productivity Software: Tools that help users produce documents, databases, graphs, and presentations.
Task Scheduling: The operating system's ability to manage the execution of multiple tasks.
User Interface: The part of the operating system that allows users to interact with the computer, either through GUI or CLI.
System Maintenance: Utility programs that help in cleaning up unnecessary files and backing up data.
System Monitoring: Utilities that monitor system resources and performance.
File Management: Tools designed to manage files and directories beyond capabilities provided by the operating system.
Previous Year Solved Question Paper

1. Differentiate between Application and System software. [Anna University BE/BTech 2014]
ANS: Application Software:
Purpose: Helps users perform specific tasks.
Examples: Microsoft Word, Adobe Photoshop, Google Chrome.
Interaction with Hardware: Indirect, via system software.
User Interaction: Direct.
Installation: User-installed and updated.
Categories: Business software, multimedia software, educational software.
System Software:
Purpose: Manages and controls hardware, provides a platform for application software.
Examples: Windows, macOS, Linux, device drivers.
Interaction with Hardware: Direct.

User Interaction: Indirect.

Installation: Pre-installed, updated via the operating system.

Categories: Operating systems, device drivers, utility programs.

Previous Year Unsolved Question Paper

1. What is software? Describe different software. [Anna University BE/BTech 2014]
2. Explain why an operating system is needed in a computer system. Differentiate between the system software and application software. [IGNOU BCA 2023]

Exercise

Exercise 1 – Multiple Choice Questions

1. What is the primary role of system software?
   A) Data analysis
   B) Managing hardware resources
   C) Entertainment
   D) Internet browsing

2. Which of the following is NOT an example of application software?
   A) Linux
   B) Microsoft Office
   C) Adobe Photoshop
   D) Mozilla Firefox

3. What does an operating system manage?
   A) Only software resources
   B) Only user interfaces
   C) Hardware and software resources
   D) Only internet connections

4. Which is a function of utility programs?
   A) Creating graphics
   B) Managing computer resources

C) Browsing the web

D) Word processing

5. Which software is used to interact with hardware devices directly?

A) Device Drivers

B) Operating Systems

C) Media Software

D) Web Browsers

Exercise 2 – True/False

1. Operating systems manage both hardware and software resources.
2. Utility programs are a type of application software.
3. Machine language is easy to understand and use by programmers.
4. Antivirus software is considered a utility program.
5. Database software is used for browsing the internet.

Exercise 3 – Fill in the blanks

1. The operating system provides a _______ for users to interact with the system, either through GUI or CLI.
2. Utility programs enhance and optimize the operations of the _______.
3. High-level languages are designed to be more _______ than low-level languages.
4. Machine language consists entirely of _______ and is the most basic form of instruction a computer can execute.
5. Productivity software like Microsoft Office is used to create _______.

Exercise 4- Rearrange the sentence

1. system resources efficiently manage system software is designed to
2. performing specific tasks application software is used for such as productivity or data management
3. and provides common services hardware resources that manages computer an operating system is the software
4. users to store systems allow database software and extract information from a database
5. machine code assembly language requires an assembler to convert it into

Exercise 5- Small Answers

1. What is the main function of an operating system?
2. How do device drivers function within a computer system?
3. What role do utility programs play in the maintenance of a computer system?
4. Describe the purpose of web browsers.
5. What is meant by 'task scheduling' in operating systems?

Exercise 6- Long Answers

1. Discuss how operating systems manage hardware resources.
2. Explain the different types of application software and give examples of each.

ANSWER

Exercise 1- 1) b , 2) a , 3) c , 4) b , 5) a
Exercise 2- 1) True , 2) False , 3) False , 4) True , 5) False
Exercise 3- 1) interface , 2) operating system , 3) abstract , 4) binary code , 5) documents
Exercise 4- 1) System software is designed to manage system resources efficiently.
2) Application software is used for performing specific tasks such as productivity or data management.
3) An operating system is the software that manages computer hardware resources and provides common services.
4) Database software systems allow users to store and extract information from a database.
5) Assembly language requires an assembler to convert it into machine code.

Exercise 5-
1. The CPU (Central Processing Unit) executes instructions and processes data, functioning as the brain of the computer.
2. They facilitate communication between the operating system and hardware devices, making it possible for software applications to use the hardware functionality without needing to know precise details about the hardware being used.
3. They help manage, maintain, and control computer resources, such as by cleaning up unnecessary files, defragmenting disks, and scanning for malware.
4. Web browsers enable users to access and navigate the internet, displaying web pages and handling web-based data.
5. Task scheduling refers to the way an operating system manages the execution of multiple tasks, allocating processor time to ensure that tasks are completed efficiently.

Chapter-3
TEST PAPER
Introduction to Computers

Time Duration: 30 Minutes **Maximum Marks: 25**

General Instructions:

1. The question paper consists of questions divided into three sections, A, B and C.
2. All questions are compulsory.
3. Section A comprises MCQs , Fill in the blanks of one mark each.
4. Section B comprises question numbers 1 to 5. These are Short Question carrying two marks each.
5. Section D comprises question numbers 1. These are Long Question carrying five marks each.

SECTION-A

Fill in the blanks- **(1 X 5 = 5 marks)**

1. Utility software helps to optimize and maintain the computer system by managing system _______.
2. The primary role of _______ is to manage tasks and resources in a computer system.
3. Adobe Photoshop is an example of _______ software, used for graphic design.
4. Programming languages that are easy to understand and use are called _______ languages.
5. Web browsers enable users to _______ websites and access internet content.

MCQ- **(1 X 5 = 5 marks)**

1. Which component is not considered system software?
A) Operating System
B) Microsoft Excel
C) Device Driver
D) Utility Program

2. What is the primary function of device drivers?
A) To provide internet access

B) To manage files and folders
C) To facilitate communication between hardware and software
D) To enhance graphical performance

3. Which of the following is a feature of high-level programming languages?
A) They require detailed knowledge of hardware architecture.
B) They operate dirctly on the hardware.
C) They make the programming process easier and more efficient.
D) They are written in binary code.

4. Which utility program is commonly used to prevent and remove malware?
A) File manager
B) Disk defragmenter
C) Antivirus program
D) Web browser

5. What type of software would be used to create databases?
A) Operating system
B) Utility software
C) Device driver
D) Database software

SECTION-B

Short Question- **(2 X 5 = 10 marks)**

1. What is the main purpose of an operating system?
2. Describe one function of utility programs.
3. What does a device driver do in a computer system?
4. Name a type of application software and its purpose.
5. Why are high-level programming languages preferred over low-level languages for general application development?

SECTION-C

Long Question- **(5 X 1 = 5 marks)**

1. Discuss the differences between system software and application software, including examples and roles of each.

ONLINE RESOURCES

Chapter 3 Practice Paper
Link: https://forms.gle/SzevWcRW8xwQr1Vg6
QR Code:

Chapter 3 Video Content
Link: https://youtu.be/FIlJlH03CR4?si=mU0vkvrwC4QJqOzD
QR Code:

Chapter 4: Data Representation and Processing

In this chapter you will learn about:

Number Systems
Binary Arithmetic and Logic Operations
Data Representation
Understanding Boolean Algebra and Logic Gates

In the world of computers, understanding number systems is fundamental, and this knowledge serves as the foundation for various aspects of computing. This chapter delves into the intricacies of number systems, computer software, and programming languages.

4.1 Number Systems:

The digital realm of computers revolves around the concept of number systems. At its core, a computer processes information in the form of binary digits, or bits, which are either 0s or 1s. This section introduces you to the basic principles of number systems and their significance in computing. Number systems are the means by which we represent and manipulate data in a digital format. We'll explore why computers primarily use the binary number system, how other bases like octal and hexadecimal fit into the equation, and why these systems are crucial for representing data in computers. Understanding these systems lays the groundwork for comprehending how computers store and process information.

Binary, Octal, and Hexadecimal Number Bases:

Binary/Decimal																
Bit #	15	14	13	12	11	10	9	8	7	6	5	4	3	2	1	0
Power	2^{15}	2^{14}	2^{13}	2^{12}	2^{11}	2^{10}	2^9	2^8	2^7	2^6	2^5	2^4	2^3	2^2	2^1	2^0
Decimal Bit Value	32678	16284	8192	4096	2048	1024	512	256	128	64	32	16	8	4	2	1
Max Value	65535_{10}															
Hexadecimal																
Bit #	15	14	13	12	11	10	9	8	7	6	5	4	3	2	1	0
Power	16^3				16^2				16^1				16^0			
Decimal Bit Value	8	4	2	1	8	4	2	1	8	4	2	1	8	4	2	1
Max Value	F				F				F				F			
BCD																
Bit #	15	14	13	12	11	10	9	8	7	6	5	4	3	2	1	0
Power	10^3				10^2				10^1				10^0			
Decimal Bit Value	8	4	2	1	8	4	2	1	8	4	2	1	8	4	2	1
Max Value	9				9				9				9			
Octal																
Bit #	15	14	13	12	11	10	9	8	7	6	5	4	3	2	1	0
Power	8^5	8^4			8^3			8^2			8^1			8^0		
Decimal Bit Value	1	4	2	1	4	2	1	4	2	1	4	2	1	4	2	1
Max Value	1	7			7			7			7			7		
Real (Floating Point 32)																
Bit #	31	30	29	28	27	26	25	24	23	22	21	20	19	18	17	16
	Sign	Exponent								Mantissa						
Bit #	15	14	13	12	11	10	9	8	7	6	5	4	3	2	1	0
Mantissa																

Table 8

In the digital world, binary is king. Computers, with their electronic circuits, operate most efficiently when dealing with binary digits. This section takes a deeper dive into binary and introduces two other essential number bases: octal and hexadecimal.

Binary, the base2 system, consists of only two digits: 0 and 1. We'll explore how binary numbers are used to represent information in computers, from digital logic gates to memory storage.

Octal, the base8 system, uses eight digits: 0 to 7. It's often employed in computing for its convenience in representing binary values concisely. We'll delve into the conversion between binary and octal, demonstrating how octal is useful for simplifying long binary strings. Hexadecimal, the base16 system, is favoured for its ability to compactly represent binary data. With sixteen digits (09 and AF), hexadecimal is vital for addressing memory locations and specifying colours in web design. We'll show you how hexadecimal relates to binary and how it's utilized in computing.

Binary, Octal, and Hexadecimal Number Bases: Understanding the Fundamentals Number systems are the foundation of mathematics and computing, serving as the language that computers use to process information. While the decimal system (base 10) is the most familiar to us, computers primarily use binary (base 2) as their native number system. However, there are alternative number bases, such as octal (base 8) and hexadecimal (base 16), that are frequently employed in various aspects of computing. In this comprehensive guide, we will explore binary, octal, and hexadecimal number systems, understand their fundamentals, and examine their applications in computer science.

4.1.1 Binary Number System (Base 2):

Fundamentals: The binary number system uses only two digits, 0 and 1, to represent numbers. Each digit is called a "bit," which is short for "binary digit." In binary, the value of each position is a power of 2. The rightmost bit represents 2^0 (1), the next bit to the left represents 2^1 (2), the next 2^2 (4), and so on. Binary numbers are read from right to left, just like decimal numbers.

Conversion: To convert a decimal number to binary, you repeatedly divide the decimal number by 2 and record the remainders. The binary representation is obtained by reading the remainders from bottom to top. For example, to convert 13 to binary:

13 ÷ 2 = 6 remainder 1

6 ÷ 2 = 3 remainder 0

3 ÷ 2 = 1 remainder 1

1 ÷ 2 = 0 remainder

Reading the remainders from bottom to top gives the binary representation 1101.

Applications: Binary is fundamental in computer systems because electronic circuits can easily represent two states (on/off, 0/1). Binary is used to encode and process all data within a computer, from numeric values to text, images, and program instructions.

4.1.2 Octal Number System (Base 8):

Fundamentals: The octal number system uses eight digits, 0 to 7, to represent numbers. Each digit represents a power of 8, similar to how decimal digits represent powers of 10. The rightmost digit represents 8^0 (1), the next digit to the left represents 8^1 (8), the next 8^2 (64), and so on.

Conversion: To convert a decimal number to octal, you repeatedly divide the decimal number by 8 and record the remainders. The octal representation is obtained by reading the remainders from bottom to top. For example, to convert 73 to octal:

73 ÷ 8 = 9 remainder 1

9 ÷ 8 = 1 remainder 1

1 ÷ 8 = 0 remainder 1

Reading the remainders from bottom to top gives the octal representation 111.

Applications: Octal is not commonly used in modern computing for representing numeric values. However, it was historically used in early computer systems because it aligns well with the way data is stored in binary. For example, three octal digits can represent exactly one byte (8 bits).

4.1.3 Hexadecimal Number System (Base 16):

Fundamentals: The hexadecimal number system uses sixteen digits, 0 to 9 and A to F, to represent numbers. In hexadecimal, the rightmost digit represents 16^0 (1), the next digit to the left represents 16^1 (16), the next 16^2 (256), and so on. The letters A to F are used to represent values 10 to 15, respectively.

Conversion: To convert a decimal number to hexadecimal, you repeatedly divide the decimal number by 16 and record the remainders. The hexadecimal representation is obtained by reading the remainders from bottom to top and replacing values 10 to 15 with the corresponding letters A to F. For example, to convert 255 to hexadecimal:

255 ÷ 16 = 15 remainder 15 (which is represented as F)

15 ÷ 16 = 0 remainder 15 (F again)

Reading the remainders from bottom to top gives the hexadecimal representation FF.

Applications: Hexadecimal is widely used in computer science and programming for several reasons: It is a convenient way to represent binary data in a more compact and readable form. Each hexadecimal digit corresponds

to exactly 4 binary bits, making it easy to group binary data. Memory addresses in computer systems are often expressed in hexadecimal. It is used in programming to represent colours in web design and graphics. For example, the colour FF0000 represents pure red in hexadecimal notation. Hexadecimal is frequently used in debugging and low-level programming to examine and manipulate binary data.

Binary, Octal, and Hexadecimal Interactions:

Binary to Octal and Hexadecimal: Converting from binary to octal or hexadecimal is straightforward. Group binary bits into sets of three (for octal) or four (for hexadecimal) from right to left, and then convert each group to the corresponding octal or hexadecimal digit.

Example: Binary (101110110111) to Octal:

101 110 110 111

5 6 6 7

Example: Binary (101110110111) to Hexadecimal:

1011 1011 0111

B B 7 Octal and Hexadecimal to Binary: To convert from octal or hexadecimal to binary, replace each octal digit with its three corresponding binary bits or each hexadecimal digit with its four corresponding binary bits.

Example: Octal (567) to Binary:

5 > 101

6 > 110

7 > 111 Example: Hexadecimal (1A3) to Binary:

1 > 0001

A > 1010

3 > 0011

Hexadecimal to Octal: To convert from hexadecimal to octal, first convert the hexadecimal number to binary and then group the binary bits into sets of three from right to left.

Example: Hexadecimal (1A3) to Octal:

Hex (1A3) > Binary (000110100011)

000 110 100 011 > Octal (0343)

Applications in Computer Science:

Memory Addresses: Memory addresses in computer systems are often represented in hexadecimal. For example, 0x7FFF is a hexadecimal memory address.

Data Representation: Hexadecimal is commonly used to represent binary data, such as machine code instructions and file formats, in a more readable form for debugging and analysis.

Colour Representation: In web design and graphics, colours are often represented in hexadecimal notation. For instance, the colour 00FF00 represents pure green.

Programming and Debugging: Programmers frequently use hexadecimal when working with low level programming, debugging, and examining memory dumps.

Network Addresses: In networking, IPv6 addresses are typically expressed in hexadecimal.

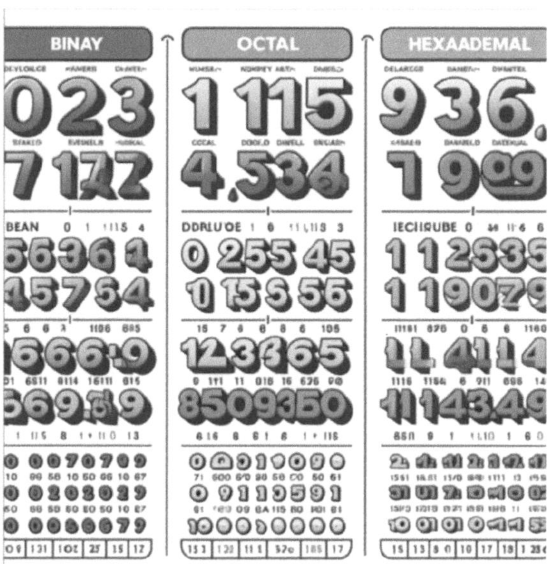

4.2 Binary Arithmetic and Logic Operations

4.2.1 Binary Addition

Binary addition works like decimal addition but has only two digits.

Example:

1011 (binary for 11)

+1101(binary for 13)

11000(binary for 24)

4.2.2 Binary Subtraction

Binary subtraction uses the method of complements for simplicity.

Example:

1100 (binary for 12)

−101(binary for 5)

0111(binary for 7)

4.2.3 Binary Multiplication

Binary multiplication is simpler than decimal multiplication, using only 0s and 1s.

Example:

101 (binary for 5)

*11 (binary for 3)

1111 (binary for 15)

4.3 Data Representation

4.3.1 Bits and Bytes

A bit is the smallest unit of data in computing. A byte consists of 8 bits.

4.3.2 ASCII

The American Standard Code for Information Interchange (ASCII) uses 7 bits to represent characters.

Example:

The ASCII code for 'A' is 65.

4.3.3 Unicode

Unicode is a universal character encoding standard that uses multiple bytes to represent all characters and symbols in all writing systems.

Example:

The Unicode for 'A' is U+0041.

4.4 Understanding Boolean Algebra and Logic Gates

4.4.1 AND Gate

The output is high (1) only if all inputs are high (1).

Input: 0, 0 → Output: 0

Input: 0, 1 → Output: 0

Input: 1, 0 → Output: 0

Input: 1, 1 → Output: 1

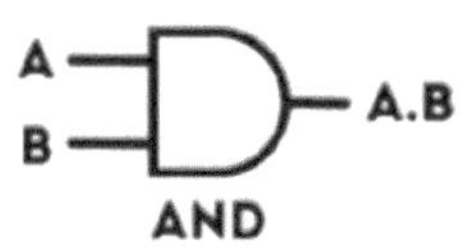

2 input AND Gate

A	B	A.B
0	0	0
0	1	0
1	0	0
1	1	1

4.4.2 OR Gate

The output is high (1) if any of the inputs are high (1).

Input: 0, 0 → Output: 0

Input: 0, 1 → Output: 1

Input: 1, 0 → Output: 1

Input: 1, 1 → Output: 1

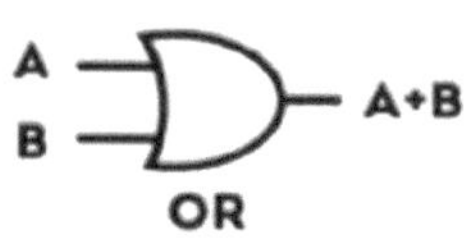

2 input OR Gate

A	B	A+B
0	0	0
0	1	1
1	0	1
1	1	1

4.4.3 NOT Gate

The output is the inverse of the input.

NOT Gate

A	Ā
0	1
1	0

4.4.4 NAND Gate

The output is the inverse of the AND gate.

4.4.5 NOR Gate

The output is the inverse of the OR gate.

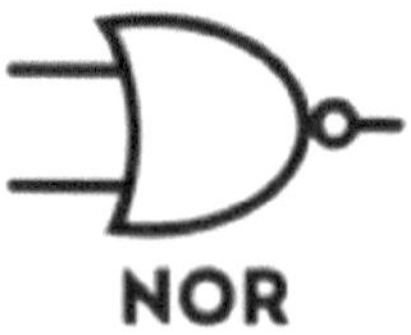

4.4.6 EX-OR Gate

The output is high (1) only if the inputs are different.

Summary

Computers use binary (base-2) as their primary language, but octal (base-8) and hexadecimal (base-16) are also important for simplifying data representation and addressing in computing.

Adds two binary numbers and carries over as needed (e.g., 11 + 13 = 24 in binary).

Uses the method of complements.

Multiplication of binary numbers simplifies to addition based on 0s and 1s.

The fundamental units of data in computing, with one byte consisting of eight bits.

Standards for encoding characters, with ASCII using 7 bits and Unicode using multiple bytes to encompass all written languages.
Fundamental gates that perform basic logic functions.
Variations that provide inverse or exclusive outputs, critical for complex logic circuits.
Often done in hexadecimal for efficiency and readability.
Hexadecimal is widely used for these purposes, particularly in web design and programming.

Glossary

Binary Number System (Base 2): A number system that uses only two digits, 0 and 1, to represent numbers. Each position represents a power of 2.
Octal Number System (Base 8): A number system that uses eight digits, 0 to 7, to represent numbers. Each position represents a power of 8.
Hexadecimal Number System (Base 16): A number system that uses sixteen digits, 0 to 9 and A to F, to represent numbers. Each position represents a power of 16.
Bit: The smallest unit of data in computing, representing a single binary digit (0 or 1).
Byte: A group of 8 bits.
ASCII: American Standard Code for Information Interchange, a character encoding standard using 7 bits to represent characters.
Unicode: A universal character encoding standard using multiple bytes to represent all characters and symbols in all writing systems.
Memory Addresses: Locations in computer memory often represented in hexadecimal.
Network Addresses: IP addresses in networking, often expressed in hexadecimal.

Previous Year Unsolved Question Paper

1. Write full form of BCD and ASCII [IGNOU BCA 2023]

ANS: BCD: Binary-Coded Decimal

ASCII: American Standard Code for Information Interchange

2. What are the different symbols used in the hexadecimal number system?[Anna University BE/BTech 2014]

ANS: The hexadecimal number system, also known as base-16, uses the following 16 symbols:

Digits 0-9:

0,1,2,3,4,5,6,7,8,9

Letters A-F (or a-f):

A (or a) represents the decimal value 10

B (or b) represents the decimal value 11

C (or c) represents the decimal value 12

D (or d) represents the decimal value 13

E (or e) represents the decimal value 14

F (or f) represents the decimal value 15

Summary of Hexadecimal Symbols

Digits: 0, 1, 2, 3, 4, 5, 6, 7, 8, 9

Letters: A, B, C, D, E, F (uppercase) or a, b, c, d, e, f (lowercase)

These symbols are used to represent values in the hexadecimal system, where each digit's place value is a power of 16.

Previous Year Unsolved Question Paper

1. Differentiate ASCII and extended ASCII.[Anna University BE/BTech 2014]

Exercise

Exercise 1 – Multiple Choice Questions

1. What is the base number of the binary system?**
   A) 10
   B) 2
   C) 8
   D) 16

2. Which number system is used primarily for memory addressing by programmers?
   A) Decimal
   B) Binary
   C) Octal
   D) Hexadecimal

3. What does each hexadecimal digit represent in binary digits?
   A) 2 bits
   B) 4 bits
   C) 8 bits
   D) 16 bits

4. Which of the following is a use of the octal number system in computing?
   A) User interface design
   B) Memory addressing
   C) Simplifying binary representation
   D) Network configuration

5. Binary addition of 1011 and 1101 results in:
   A) 11000
   B) 10110
   C) 10010
   D) 11111

Exercise 2 – True/False

1. Binary is the only number system used in computing.
2. Hexadecimal digits include numbers from 0-9 and letters from A-F.
3. A byte consists of 16 bits.
4. Unicode uses 7 bits to represent each character.
5. The AND gate outputs high only if all inputs are low.

Exercise 3 – Fill in the blanks

1. Binary number system uses digits 0 and ___.
2. The octal number system is base ___.
3. Hexadecimal numbers include digits from 0 to 9 and letters from A to ___.
4. ASCII represents characters using __ bits.
5. In computing, a byte consists of __ bits.

Exercise 4- Choose the Odd One Out

1. Identify the odd one out:

A) Binary

B) Octal

C) Decimal

D) ASCII

2. Identify the odd one out:

A) NAND

B) NOR

C) OR

D) ASCII

3. Identify the odd one out:

A) Hexadecimal

B) Decimal

C) Unicode

D) Octal

4. Identify the odd one out:

A) Bit

B) Byte

C) Nibble

D) Pixel

5. Identify the odd one out:

A) 1010 (binary)

B) 12 (octal)

C) 0A (hexadecimal)

D) 100 (decimal)

Exercise 5- Small Answers

1. What is the significance of the binary number system in computing?
2. Explain the process of converting a decimal number to binary.
3. Why is the hexadecimal system used in computer science?
4. What is the role of ASCII in data representation?
5. Describe the function of the AND gate in logic circuits.

Exercise 6- Long Answers

1. Discuss the importance of understanding different number systems in computing.
2. Explain the conversion methods between binary, octal, and hexadecimal number systems with examples.

Answers

Exercise 1- 1) B , 2) D , 3) B , 4) C , 5) A
Exercise 2- 1) False , 2) True , 3) False , 4) False , 5) False
Exercise 3- 1) 2 , 2) 8 , 3) F , 4) 7 , 5) 8
Exercise 4- 1) D , 2) D , 3) C , 4) D , 5) D
Exercise 5- 1) The binary number system is fundamental in computing because it represents data using only two digits (0 and 1), which align with the on/off states of electronic circuits, enabling efficient data processing and storage.
2) To convert a decimal number to binary, repeatedly divide the decimal number by 2 and record the remainders. The binary representation is obtained by reading the remainders from bottom to top.
3) The hexadecimal system is used because it provides a more compact and readable representation of binary data, simplifies the notation of large binary numbers, and is commonly used in memory addressing and programming.
4) ASCII is a character encoding standard that uses 7 bits to represent text characters and control codes, allowing for consistent representation and communication of text data across different systems.
5) The AND gate outputs a high signal (1) only if all its inputs are high (1). Otherwise, it outputs a low signal (0).

Chapter-4
TEST PAPER
Introduction to Computers

Time Duration: 30 Minutes **Maximum Marks: 25**

General Instructions:

1. The question paper consists of different type of questions divided into three sections, A, B and C.
2. All questions are compulsory.
3. Section A comprises Fill in the blanks and True/False of one mark each.
4. Section B comprises question numbers 1 to 5. These are Short Question carrying two marks each.
5. Section D comprises question numbers 1. These are Long Question carrying five marks each.

SECTION-A

Fill in the blanks- **(1 X 5 = 5 marks)**

1. The binary number system is also known as the base-_______________ system.
2. In the hexadecimal system, the letter 'B' represents the decimal number _________________.
3. The process of converting binary data into octal or hexadecimal is known as _____________.
4. A byte, which is composed of 8 bits, can represent ______________ different values.
5. The OR gate outputs high (1) if _____________ of its inputs are high (1).

True/False- **(1 X 5 = 5 marks)**

1. Binary numbers are read from left to right, just like decimal numbers.
2. In binary addition, 1 + 1 equals 10, which results in a carry.
3. Octal number system is frequently used in modern computer systems for representing colors in web design.
4. ASCII and Unicode both provide standards for text encoding, but Unicode supports a broader range of characters.
5. A NAND gate produces a low output only if all its inputs are high.

SECTION-B

Short Question- **(2 X 5 = 10 marks)**

1. What is the primary advantage of using hexadecimal over binary for data representation?
2. Explain the relationship between binary and octal number systems.
3. What is the role of Boolean algebra in designing digital circuits?
4. How does the ASCII standard represent characters?
5. Describe the function of an XOR gate in a digital circuit.

SECTION-C

Long Question- **(5 X 1 = 5 marks)**

1. Discuss the significance of number systems in computing, particularly focusing on binary, octal, and hexadecimal systems. Explain their fundamental principles, conversions between these systems, and their practical applications in computer science.

ONLINE RESOURCES

Chapter 4 Practice Paper
Link: https://forms.gle/gAMBtzzHYXDTcw4f9
QR Code:

Chapter 4 Practice Paper
Link: https://youtu.be/YR1oXj-JtE8?si=gP4vaXBBRwuHMiHn
QR Code:

Chapter 5: Computer Networks

In this chapter you will learn about :

History and Evolution of the Internet
Types of Networks
Basics of Networking and Data Communication
Network Topologies and Protocols

5.1 History and Evolution of the Internet

5.1.1 The Beginning

The history of the internet begins in the late 1960s with the creation of ARPANET by the Defense Advanced Research Projects Agency (DARPA) in the United States. ARPANET was the first network to implement the protocol suite TCP/IP, which paved the way for modern internet communication.

5.1.2 Expansion and Commercialization

Throughout the 1980s and 1990s, the internet experienced rapid expansion and was adopted for civilian and commercial uses. This era saw the introduction of the World Wide Web in 1991 by Tim Berners-Lee, which revolutionized how information was shared and accessed.

5.1.3 Modern Internet

Today, the internet is a global system of interconnected computer networks that utilize the Internet protocol suite (TCP/IP) to link devices worldwide. It's a network of networks that consists of private, public, academic, business, and government networks.

5.2 Basics of Networking and Data Communication

5.2.1 Networking Basics

Networking involves connecting two or more computers or devices to share resources, exchange files, or allow electronic communications. Networks can be as simple as two computers connected via Bluetooth or as complex as the global internet.

5.2.2 Data Communication

Data communication refers to the transmission of digital data between two or more computers or devices. The effectiveness of a data communication system is measured by throughput, transmission speed, latency, and error rate.

5.3 Types of Networks

5.3.1 Local Area Network (LAN)

A LAN connects computers within a relatively small area, such as a home, school, or office building. LANs are known for their high data transfer rates and low latency.

Example: A business office network connecting all computers to a single server and multiple printers.

5.3.2 Wide Area Network (WAN)

A WAN spans a large geographic area, such as a city, country, or the entire globe. The internet is the largest WAN, comprising many interconnected LANs and MANs.

Example: A multinational corporation's network that connects its various branches across different countries using leased lines.

5.3.3 Metropolitan Area Network (MAN)

A MAN is larger than a LAN but smaller than a WAN. It covers a city or a large campus.

Example: A university campus network that connects various buildings within the campus to each other and the internet.

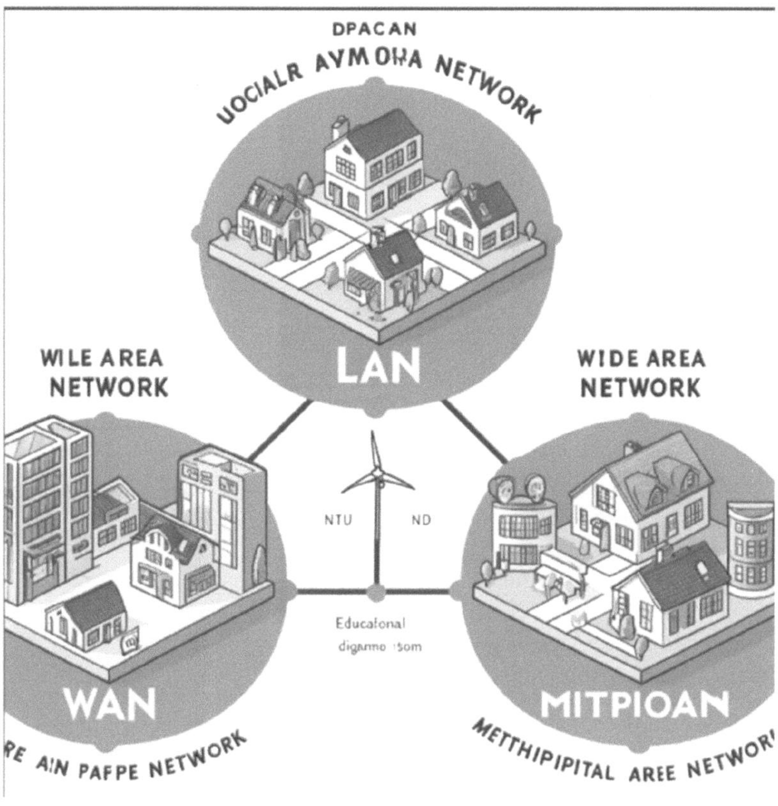

5.4 Network Topologies and Protocols

5.4.1 Network Topologies

Network topology refers to the arrangement of a network, including its nodes and connecting lines.

There are several topologies:

Bus: All devices share a single communication line.

Star: All devices are connected to a single central hub.

Ring: Each device is connected to two others, forming a ring.

Mesh: Devices are interconnected with many redundant interconnections between network nodes.

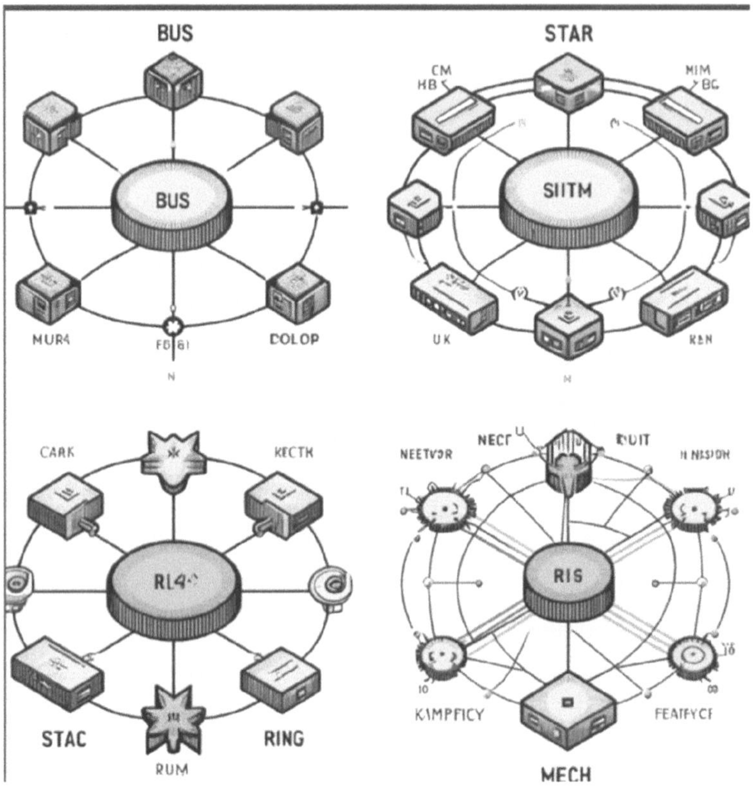

5.4.2 Network Protocols

Network protocols are formal standards and policies comprised of rules, procedures, and formats that define communication between two or more devices over a network. Key protocols include:

TCP/IP (Transmission Control Protocol/Internet Protocol): Directs how data is packaged and transmitted over the internet.

HTTP (Hypertext Transfer Protocol): Used for transferring web pages.

FTP (File Transfer Protocol): Used for transferring files between computers on a network.

Summary

Began with ARPANET in the 1960s.

Expanded and commercialized in the 1980s and 1990s with the advent of TCP/IP and the World Wide Web.

Evolved into a global network connecting diverse types of networks.

Involves connecting devices to share resources and data.

Data communication metrics include throughput, speed, latency, and error rate.
LAN (Local Area Network): Connects devices within a small area like a home or office.
WAN (Wide Area Network): Covers broad areas such as cities or countries, with the internet being the largest example.
MAN (Metropolitan Area Network): Spans larger areas than LANs but smaller than WANs, like a city or campus.

Glossary

ARPANET: Advanced Research Projects Agency Network, the early form of the internet.
TCP/IP: Transmission Control Protocol/Internet Protocol, a suite of communication protocols used to interconnect network devices on the internet.
LAN: Local Area Network, a network that connects devices within a small geographic area.
WAN: Wide Area Network, a network that extends over a large geographic area.
MAN: Metropolitan Area Network, a network designed to cover an area of the size of a metropolitan area.
Bus Topology: A network setup where each device is connected to a single central cable or bus.
Star Topology: A network setup where all devices are connected to a single central device.
Ring Topology: A network configuration where each device is connected to two other devices, forming a circular data path.
Mesh Topology: A network setup where devices are interconnected with many redundant interconnections.
HTTP: Hypertext Transfer Protocol, used for transmitting web pages over the internet.
FTP: File Transfer Protocol, a standard network protocol used for the transfer of computer files between a client and server on a computer network.

Previous Year Solved Question Paper

1. Compare LAN, WAN and MAN. Give characteristics of each, with suitable example. [IGNOU CIT 2023]
ANS: Local Area Network (LAN), Metropolitan Area Network (MAN), and Wide Area Network (WAN) are different types of networks that vary in terms of geographic coverage, speed, cost, and usage. Here is a detailed comparison of their characteristics:
Local Area Network (LAN)
Geographic Scope: Covers a small geographic area such as a single building, office, or campus.
Speed: Typically high-speed, ranging from 100 Mbps to 10 Gbps.

Cost: Lower cost compared to MAN and WAN, due to the limited area and infrastructure required.
Setup and Maintenance: Easier to set up and maintain.
Ownership: Usually owned, operated, and maintained by a single organization or individual.
Usage: Commonly used within homes, small businesses, schools, and small campuses.
Example: A network within a single office building connecting computers, printers, and other devices.

Metropolitan Area Network (MAN)
Geographic Scope: Covers a larger geographic area than a LAN, such as a city or a large campus.
Speed: Moderate to high speed, generally ranging from 1 Mbps to 1 Gbps.
Cost: Higher cost than LAN due to the broader coverage and more complex infrastructure.
Setup and Maintenance: More complex setup and maintenance than LAN, often requiring specialized personnel.
Ownership: May be owned and operated by a single organization or a consortium of organizations, often involving telecom providers.
Usage: Used to connect multiple LANs within a city, providing efficient and high-speed connectivity.
Example: A network connecting various branches of a university across a city.

Wide Area Network (WAN)
Geographic Scope: Covers a very large geographic area, potentially global.
Speed: Varies widely, from lower speeds (56 Kbps) to high speeds (100 Gbps) depending on the technology and infrastructure used.
Cost: Highest cost among the three types of networks due to extensive coverage and the need for sophisticated infrastructure.
Setup and Maintenance: Most complex setup and maintenance, often involving multiple service providers and international regulations.
Ownership: Typically owned by multiple organizations, including telecom companies and service providers. Usage is often on a subscription or lease basis.
Usage: Used to connect LANs and MANs over long distances, enabling communication and data sharing across cities, countries, and continents.
Example: The internet is the largest example of a WAN, connecting millions of LANs and other networks worldwide.

Previous Year Unsolved Question Paper

1. Explain the roles and responsibilities of a Network Administrator. [IGNOU BCA 2023]
2. Explain different Network Topologies.[IGNOU MCA 2023]

Exercise

Exercise 1 – Multiple Choice Questions

1. What was the original name of the early form of the internet?
   A) World Wide Web
   B) ARPANET
   C) TCP/IP
   D) Ethernet

2. Who introduced the World Wide Web in 1991?
   A) Vint Cerf
   B) Larry Page
   C) Tim Berners-Lee
   D) Steve Jobs

3. Which protocol suite is fundamental to internet communication?
   A) HTTP
   B) FTP
   C) TCP/IP
   D) SMTP

4. What is the primary purpose of a LAN?
   A) To connect devices across the globe
   B) To connect devices within a small geographic area
   C) To connect devices within a city
   D) To connect devices within a country

5. What does WAN stand for?
   A) Wide Area Network
   B) World Area Network
   C) Web Area Network
   D) Wireless Area Network

Exercise 2 – True/False

1. ARPANET was developed by NASA.

2. TCP/IP is a suite of communication protocols used on the internet.

3. A Local Area Network (LAN) covers a larger geographic area than a Wide Area Network (WAN).

4. HTTP is used for transferring web pages over the internet.

5. A ring topology connects all devices to a single central hub.

Exercise 3 – Fill in the blanks

1. The creation of ARPANET by DARPA in the 1960s marked the beginning of the ____.
2. The World Wide Web was introduced by Tim Berners-Lee in ____.
3. A LAN typically has high data transfer rates and low ____.
4. WANs often use __ lines to connect different branches across countries.
5. In a star topology, all devices are connected to a single central ____.

Exercise 4- Jumble words

1. RPANETA
2. CORMALIMEZON
3. OLYPOTOG
4. YANCETL
5. KETROYWNG

Exercise 5- Small Answers

1. What was ARPANET and why was it significant?
2. Who introduced the World Wide Web and in what year?
3. What are the main functions of a Local Area Network (LAN)?
4. Explain the significance of TCP/IP in networking.
5. Describe the star topology in networking.

Exercise 6- Long Answers

1. Discuss the history and evolution of the internet from its inception to the present day.
2. Explain the differences between LAN, WAN, and MAN, providing examples of each.

Answer

Exercise 1- 1) B , 2) C , 3) C , 4) B , 5) A
Exercise 2- 1) False , 2) True , 3) False , 4) True , 5) False

Exercise 3- 1) internet , 2) 1991 , 3) latency , 4) leased , 5) hub

Exercise 4- 1) ARPANET ,
2) COMMERCIALIZE ,
3) TOPOLOGY ,
4) LATENCY,
5) NETWORKING

Exercise 5- 1) ARPANET was the first network to implement the TCP/IP protocol suite, marking the beginning of the modern internet.

2) Tim Berners-Lee introduced the World Wide Web in 1991.

3) A LAN connects devices within a small geographic area, facilitating high data transfer rates and low latency for sharing resources and electronic communications.

4) TCP/IP is a suite of communication protocols that underpin internet communication, directing how data is packaged, transmitted, and received over networks.

5) In a star topology, all devices are connected to a single central hub, which facilitates communication between the connected devices.

Chapter-5
TEST PAPER
Introduction to Computers

Time Duration: 30 Minutes **Maximum Marks: 25**

General Instructions:

1. The question paper consists of questions and is divided into three sections, A, B and C.
2. All questions are compulsory.
3. Section A comprises Fill in the blanks and True/False of one mark each.
4. Section B comprises question numbers 1 to 5. These are Short Question carrying two marks each.
5. Section C comprises question numbers 1. These are Long Question carrying five marks each.

SECTION-A

Fill in the blanks- **(1 X 5 = 5 marks)**

1. The ARPANET was created by the ______ in the late 1960s.
2. The World Wide Web, introduced by Tim Berners-Lee, revolutionized information sharing in ______.
3. A network protocol that is used to transfer files between computers is known as ______.
4. A ______ connects computers within a relatively small area, such as a home or office building.
5. ______ is a key metric in data communication that measures the time delay in data transmission.

True/False-

(1 X 5 = 5 marks)

1. The primary purpose of a WAN is to connect devices within a small geographic area.
2. Mesh topology provides many redundant interconnections between network nodes.
3. The HTTP protocol is used for sending emails.
4. TCP/IP is the protocol suite used to link devices worldwide.
5. A ring topology connects all devices to a single central hub.

SECTION-B

Short Question- **(2 X 5 = 10 marks)**

1. What was the significance of the ARPANET in the development of the modern internet?
2. What are the main differences between LAN and WAN?
3. How does a star topology function in a network setup?
4. Why is HTTP crucial for the World Wide Web?
5. What role does latency play in data communication?

SECTION-C

Long Question- . **(5 marks)**

1. Discuss the different types of network topologies and their advantages and disadvantages.

ONLINE RESOURCES

Chapter 5 Practice Paper
Link: https://forms.gle/SrTpuq56HooLntaH9
QR Code:

Chapter 5 Video Content
Link: https://youtu.be/9nzIdehBJ-c?si=7mqHDy3Bw1Pdz0yv
QR Code:

Chapter 6: Computer Security and Ethics

In this chapter you will learn about:

Threats to Computer Security
Security Measures and Encryption Techniques
Ethical and Legal Issues in Computing

6.1 Threats to Computer Security

6.1.1 Viruses and Malware

Viruses and malware are malicious software programs designed to damage or disrupt systems. They can delete files, steal data, or render a device unusable. Common types include ransomware, spyware, and worms.

Example: The WannaCry ransomware attack in 2017 infected hundreds of thousands of computers across 150 countries, encrypting data and demanding ransom payments in Bitcoin.

6.1.2 Hacking

Hacking involves unauthorized intrusion into computer systems by individuals or groups. Hackers might exploit vulnerabilities for various purposes: stealing corporate data, personal identities, or even just for the challenge.

Example: The Equifax data breach in 2017, where hackers accessed the personal information of approximately 147 million people, exposing social security numbers, birthdates, and other private data.

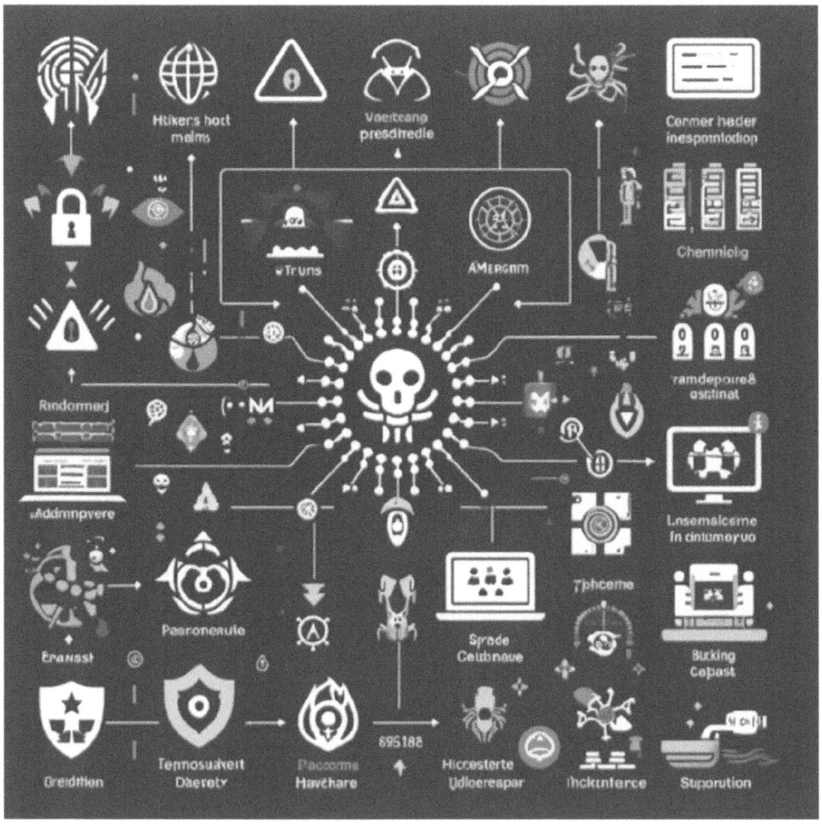

6.2 Security Measures and Encryption Techniques

6.2.1 Security Measures

Effective security measures are crucial for protecting computer systems and networks. These include:

Antivirus and Anti-malware software: Programs designed to detect and eliminate malicious software.

Firewalls: Hardware or software that blocks unauthorized access to a network.

Two-Factor Authentication (2FA): An additional layer of security requiring not only a password and username but also something that only the user has on them.

6.2.2 Encryption Techniques

Encryption is a method of protecting data by transforming it into a secure format that cannot be easily interpreted without a decryption key.

Symmetric Encryption: Uses a single key for both encryption and decryption.

Asymmetric Encryption: Uses a public key for encryption and a private key for decryption.

Example: HTTPS, the secure version of HTTP, uses encryption to secure the transfer of information between your browser and the website you are connected to.

6.3 Ethical and Legal Issues in Computing

6.3.1 Ethical Issues

Ethical issues in computing often involve questions about privacy, data security, and the responsible use of technology.

Privacy Concerns: How personal data is collected, used, and shared.

Intellectual Property: Issues surrounding the protection and theft of software, music, videos, and other digital content.

6.3.2 Legal Issues

Legal issues in computing relate to the legislation that governs the use and misuse of technology.

Data Protection Laws: Regulations that dictate how personal information must be handled; for example, the General Data Protection Regulation (GDPR) in the European Union.

Cybercrime Legislation: Laws that criminalize certain online behaviors like hacking, unauthorized access, and the distribution of malicious software.

Summary

Malicious software that harms or exploits systems, such as ransomware and spyware.
Hacking is unauthorized access to systems, often to steal data or disrupt services, as seen in major breaches like Equifax.
Security Measure include antivirus programs, firewalls, and two-factor authentication to protect against unauthorized access and attacks.
Encryption Techniques are essential for securing data, with symmetric encryption using a single key and asymmetric encryption using a pair of public and private keys.
Ethical Issues concerns about privacy, data security, and responsible tech use.
Legal Issues include data protection laws like GDPR and laws against cybercrime.

Glossary

Virus: A type of malware that replicates by copying itself to other programs, files, or computers.
Malware: Short for malicious software, designed to damage, disrupt, or gain unauthorized access to a computer system.
Ransomware: Malware that locks or encrypts data, demanding a ransom to restore access.
Spyware: Malware that secretly observes the computer user's activities without permission.
Hacking: The unauthorized intrusion into computer systems or networks.
Antivirus Software: Software designed to detect and destroy computer viruses and other malicious software.
Firewall: A security system that controls the incoming and outgoing network traffic based on predetermined security rules.
Two-Factor Authentication (2FA): A security process in which users provide two different authentication factors to verify themselves.
Symmetric Encryption: An encryption method where the same key is used for both encryption and decryption.
Asymmetric Encryption: An encryption method that uses a pair of keys, one public and one private, for encryption and decryption.
GDPR (General Data Protection Regulation): EU legislation that protects all EU citizens from privacy and data breaches in an increasingly data-driven world.
Cybercrime: Criminal activities carried out by means of computers or the internet.

Previous Year Solved Question Paper

1. Describe malware.[IGNOU MCA 2023]

ANS: Malware, short for malicious software, is any software intentionally designed to cause damage to a computer, server, client, or computer network. It can take various forms, such as viruses, worms, trojans, ransomware, spyware, adware, and more. The primary goal of malware is to disrupt operations, steal sensitive information, gain unauthorized access, or display unwanted advertisements.

2. What are the needs to regulate cyber space?[IGNOU MCA 2023]

ANS: Regulating cyberspace is essential to ensure a safe, secure, and fair online environment. Here are the key reasons why regulation is needed:

1. Security

Prevent Cyber Attacks: To protect against cyber threats such as hacking, malware, and denial-of-service attacks that can compromise sensitive data and critical infrastructure.

National Security: To safeguard national security interests, including defense systems and government operations, from cyber espionage and attacks.

2. Privacy Protection

Data Privacy: To ensure the protection of personal and sensitive information of individuals and organizations from unauthorized access and misuse.

Compliance: To enforce compliance with data protection regulations and standards (e.g., GDPR, HIPAA) that mandate how data should be collected, stored, and processed.

3. Consumer Protection

Prevent Fraud: To protect consumers from online fraud, scams, and deceptive practices.

Quality of Service: To ensure that consumers receive reliable and fair services from online providers.

4. Intellectual Property Rights

Copyright Protection: To protect intellectual property rights by preventing the illegal distribution and use of copyrighted material.

Innovation Incentives: To encourage innovation and creativity by ensuring that creators and businesses can protect and monetize their work.

5. Economic Stability

Market Integrity: To maintain the integrity of digital markets and prevent illegal activities such as money laundering and financial fraud.

Fair Competition: To promote fair competition and prevent monopolistic practices in the digital economy.

6. Ethical and Social Responsibility

Content Regulation: To regulate harmful content, including hate speech, cyberbullying, and misinformation, ensuring a safe online environment.

Digital Inclusion: To promote equitable access to digital resources and prevent digital divide issues.

7. International Cooperation

Global Standards: To establish and harmonize international standards and norms for cybersecurity, data protection, and digital trade.

Cross-Border Crime Prevention: To facilitate cooperation between countries in combating cross-border cybercrime and enforcing laws.

Previous Year Unsolved Question Paper

1. Explain the following terms: Phishing, Hacking, Ransomware [IGNOU MCA 2023]

Exercise

Exercise 1 – Multiple Choice Questions

1. What is a common type of malware that locks or encrypts data and demands a ransom to restore access?
   A) Spyware
   B) Adware
   C) Ransomware
   D) Worm

2. Which 2017 attack infected computers across 150 countries and demanded ransom payments in Bitcoin?
   A) Stuxnet
   B) WannaCry
   C) Mydoom
   D) Code Red

3. What was compromised in the Equifax data breach of 2017?
   A) Banking information
   B) Medical records
   C) Personal information including social security numbers and birthdates
   D) Credit card details

4. What is the primary function of a firewall in computer security?

A) Detect and remove viruses

B) Block unauthorized access to a network

C) Encrypt data

D) Back up data

5. Which of the following is an example of symmetric encryption?

A) RSA

B) HTTPS

C) AES

D) PG

Exercise 2 – True/False

1. Viruses and malware can steal data or render a device unusable.
2. The WannaCry attack was a type of spyware.
3. Hacking is always done for malicious purposes.
4. Firewalls are used to block unauthorized access to a network.
5. Symmetric encryption uses a pair of keys, one for encryption and one for decryption.

Exercise 3 – Fill in the blanks

1. Viruses and ______ are designed to damage or disrupt systems.
2. The WannaCry ______ attack in 2017 infected computers across 150 countries.
3. Hacking involves unauthorized ______ into computer systems.
4. Antivirus and anti-malware software are designed to detect and eliminate ______ software.
5. ______ is an additional layer of security requiring a password and something only the user has.

Exercise 4 - Match case

1. Virus - A) Encrypts data and demands ransom
2. Ransomware - B) Displays unwanted advertisements
3. Spyware - C) Replicates itself to spread across networks
4. Worm - D) Secretly observes user activities
5. Adware - E) Attaches itself to clean files and spreads

Exercise 5 - Small Answers

1. What is ransomware and how does it affect computer systems?

2. Explain the concept of Two-Factor Authentication (2FA).

3. What is the difference between symmetric and asymmetric encryption?

4. How does a firewall contribute to network security?

5. Describe the purpose of GDPR.

Exercise 6 - Long Answers

1. Discuss the various types of malware, their effects on computer systems, and methods for prevention and mitigation.

2. Explain the principles of symmetric and asymmetric encryption, providing examples of each and their applications in securing data.

Answers

Exercise 1- 1) C , 2) B , 3) C , 4) B , 5) C
Exercise 2- 1) True , 2) False , 3) False , 4) True , 5) False
Exercise 3- 1) malware , 2) ransomware , 3) intrusion , 4) malicious , 5) Two-Factor Authentication
Exercise 4- 1) - E, 2) - A, 3) - D, 4)- C, 5) - B

Exercise 5- 1)Ransomware is a type of malware that encrypts a victim's files, rendering them inaccessible, and demands payment for the decryption key to restore access.
2)Two-Factor Authentication (2FA) is a security process that requires users to provide two different authentication factors to verify their identity, enhancing security by combining something the user knows (like a password) with something the user has (like a physical token or a code sent to a mobile device).

3)Symmetric encryption uses a single key for both encryption and decryption, while asymmetric encryption uses a pair of keys – a public key for encryption and a private key for decryption.

4)A firewall controls incoming and outgoing network traffic based on predetermined security rules, blocking unauthorized access to protect the network from potential threats.

5)The General Data Protection Regulation (GDPR) is EU legislation that aims to protect personal data and privacy of EU citizens, establishing rules for data collection, storage, and processing, and imposing penalties for non-compliance.

Chapter-6
TEST PAPER
Introduction to Computers

Time Duration: 30 Minutes **Maximum Marks: 25**

General Instructions:

1. The question paper consists of questions and is divided into three sections, A, B and C.
2. All questions are compulsory.
3. Section A comprises Fill in the blanks and True/False of one mark each.
4. Section B comprises question numbers 1 to 5. These are Short Question carrying two marks each.
5. Section C comprises question numbers 1. These are Long Questions\ carrying five marks each.

SECTION-A

Fill in the blanks- **(1 X 5 = 5 marks)**

1. A ______ is a type of malware that replicates itself and spreads to other computers.
2. ______ involves unauthorized access to computer systems or networks.
3. The encryption technique that uses a pair of keys, one public and one private, is called ______ encryption.
4. ______ software is designed to detect, prevent, and remove malicious software from a computer system.
5. The General Data Protection Regulation (GDPR) was implemented to protect the data privacy of citizens in the ______ Union.

True/False- **(1 X 5 = 5 marks)**

1. Spyware is a type of malware that encrypts data and demands a ransom to unlock it.
2. Firewalls can be both hardware and software solutions for network security.
3. Symmetric encryption uses two different keys for encryption and decryption.
4. Data protection laws are designed to regulate how personal information is collected, used, and stored.
5. Cybercrime legislation includes measures against phishing attacks.

SECTION-B

Short Question- **(2 X 5 = 10 marks)**

1. What is the primary purpose of encryption in data security?
2. How do firewalls contribute to network security?
3. What ethical issues arise from the collection and use of personal data by companies?
4. Describe the role of antivirus software in protecting computer systems.
5. What are some common methods used by hackers to gain unauthorized access to computer systems?

SECTION-C

Long Question- . **(5 marks)**

1. Evaluate the impact of cybercrime legislation on combating cyber threats and enhancing cybersecurity.

NLINE RESOURCES

Chapter 6 Practice Paper
Link: https://forms.gle/1s3SFjfVmBSxTJPF9
QR Code:

Chapter 6 Video Content
Link: https://youtu.be/qA5D-TRU2RU?si=_RtV9q5yABTBb8y8
QR Code:

Chapter 7: Computer Architecture

In this chapter you will learn about:
Von Neumann Architecture
Instruction Set Architecture
Structures Interaction between Assembly and High-Level Languages

7.1 Von Neumann Architecture

Von Neumann architecture forms the core of most digital computer systems and is named after John von Neumann, a mathematician and physicist who contributed to its development in the 1940s. This architecture is based on the concept that data and programs are stored in the computer's memory, making them as accessible as data. This design contrasts with systems where instructions are hard-coded into logic circuits.

The Von Neumann architecture consists of four main components that are interconnected by a system bus:

Memory: Stores both data and instructions in a single read/write memory. This memory can be accessed using addressable locations specified in instructions.
Arithmetic Logic Unit (ALU): Responsible for carrying out all arithmetic and logical operations. The ALU uses operands and code that tells it which operations to perform.
Control Unit (CU): Extracts instructions from memory and decodes and executes them, calling on the ALU when necessary. It controls the flow of data within the computer.
Input/Output (I/O) Devices: These include devices like keyboards, mice, displays, and printers, which are connected to the computer through interfaces that are controlled by the I/O controller.

Operation Structure

In Von Neumann architecture, the CPU operates in a series of steps called the fetch-decode-execute cycle:
Fetch- The control unit retrieves an instruction from memory. The address of this instruction is determined by the program counter, which keeps track of where in the program the computer is operating.
Decode- Once fetched, the instruction is decoded by the control unit. The decoding process involves breaking down the instruction into parts that have operational meaning.

Execute- After decoding, the execute phase begins. This involves the ALU performing arithmetic or logical operations, or it could involve adjusting the program counter to a new value, loading data from memory, or writing data back to memory.

Operand Structures

Operands are the values with which the CPU performs operations. These can be constants (immediate values) or addresses pointing to memory locations. In Von Neumann architecture, operands can be accessed directly from the instruction or read from memory, depending on the instruction type.

Advantages:

Simplicity: The architecture is easy to understand and implement, which has made it a foundational model for computer design.

Flexibility: Programs stored in memory can be easily changed without altering the physical wiring of the computer.

Disadvantages:

Bottleneck: As previously mentioned, the shared bus between the data and instructions leads to operational delays.

Security: Since the same memory stores both data and instructions, malicious programs can manipulate the operation of the computer by altering stored instructions.

7.2 Instruction Set Architecture (ISA)

7.2.1 Memory Addressing

Instruction Set Architecture (ISA) defines the part of the computer architecture related to programming, including the native data types, instructions, registers, addressing modes, memory architecture, interrupt and exception handling, and external I/O. Regarding memory addressing, ISAs define:

Direct Addressing: Accessing memory directly through a constant address within the instruction.

Indirect Addressing: Using a register or a set of registers to point to the memory address.

Indexed Addressing: Combining an index register with a constant to calculate the address.

7.2.2 Operation Sequencing

ISAs determine the sequence in which operations are performed, impacting the overall performance and efficiency of the system. This includes pipelining, which allows for overlapping operation phases of multiple instructions.

7.2.3 Encoding

Encoding within an ISA refers to how instructions are represented in binary form. This includes specifying opcodes, operand specifiers, and other modifiers that instruct the CPU how to execute the instruction.

7.3 Interaction between Assembly and High-Level Languages

7.3.1 Assembly Language

Assembly language is a low-level programming language that provides a direct interface to the machine's hardware. It acts as a bridge between machine language, which consists of binary code that the hardware directly executes, and high-level programming languages, which are easier for humans to understand and use. Assembly language is specific to a computer's architecture, meaning that code written for one type of CPU may not run on another without modification.

Mnemonic Codes: Assembly language uses mnemonic codes or symbols instead of binary for operation codes (opcodes) and operands, making the code more readable for humans. For example, MOV, ADD, SUB are common mnemonics for move, add, and subtract operations.
One-to-One Correspondence: Each assembly language instruction corresponds to one machine language instruction, a characteristic known as a one-to-one correspondence. This is why assembly language is often referred to as a low-level language—it is just one step above machine language.
Hardware-Specific: Assembly code written for one type of processor won't necessarily work on another because different processors have different instruction sets.

Usage and Applications

Assembly language is used in scenarios where high control over hardware is needed or when a program must be as efficient as possible:

System Software: Operating systems and embedded systems often have components written in assembly language for speed and efficiency.
Performance-Critical Applications: In applications where execution speed is critical, such as video processing or real-time data analysis, assembly language is used to optimize performance.

Hardware Manipulation: Assembly is used to write programs that interact directly with hardware interfaces and controllers.

Advantages

Control: Provides detailed control over hardware resources, which is crucial for system programming.

Efficiency: Enables the writing of highly efficient, though hardware-specific, code.

Small Size: Generates smaller executables compared to high-level languages, important for environments with limited storage.

Disadvantages

Complexity: More difficult to learn and write correctly than high-level languages.

Maintenance: Assembly language programs can be hard to maintain and debug.

Portability: Low portability across different hardware platforms due to its close ties with the hardware architecture.

7.3.2 High-Level Languages

High-level programming languages are designed to be easily understood by humans, offering a notable level of abstraction from the computer's intricate hardware details. These languages enable programmers to write source code using logical and mathematical expressions, English-like statements, and common symbols that are familiar and easier to comprehend than the numeric codes and mnemonics used in lower-level programming languages.

Abstraction: High-level languages provide a significant abstraction from the machine's hardware. They manage memory allocation, garbage collection, and complex data structure implementations on their own, allowing developers to focus on building functionality.

Readability: The syntax of high-level languages is designed to be readable and understandable, often resembling natural language or mathematical notation, which makes the code more maintainable and accessible to new programmers.

Portability: Unlike assembly languages, which are often hardware-specific, high-level languages are portable across multiple platforms. This is largely because they are translated into machine code that the specific system's processor can understand, typically through compilation or interpretation.

Some popular high-level programming languages include:

Python: Known for its simplicity and readability, often used for web development, data analysis, artificial intelligence, and scientific computing.

Java: Widely used for building enterprise-scale applications, Android apps, and large systems.

C++: An extension of the C language that includes object-oriented features, making it suitable for systems programming, games development, and applications requiring real-time processing.
JavaScript: Essential for web development, used to create interactive effects within web browsers.

Advantages

Ease of Use: High-level languages are user-friendly, with clear and concise syntax.
Faster Development: Programs can be written, tested, and debugged faster than lower-level languages.
Software Quality: Enhanced readability and maintainability lead to fewer bugs and more robust software.

Disadvantages

Performance: High-level languages may not be as fast or efficient as lower-level languages since additional abstraction can lead to slower execution and more resource consumption.
Less Control: Programmers have less control over system resources like memory and processing power, which can be a critical factor in systems where efficiency is paramount.

Summary

Centralized architecture where data and programs are stored in the same memory.
Operates based on the fetch-decode-execute cycle.
Consists of Memory, ALU, Control Unit, and I/O Devices.
Key characteristics include simplicity and flexibility.
Challenges include the Von Neumann bottleneck and security vulnerabilities due to shared memory for data and instructions.
Memory addressing includes direct, indirect, and indexed addressing.
Operation sequencing may utilize techniques like pipelining to enhance performance.
Encoding specifies how instructions are represented in binary form.
Assembly language provides a direct interface to machine hardware, using mnemonic codes for operations.
High-level languages offer a greater level of abstraction, focusing on ease of use, portability, and readability.

Glossary

Direct Addressing: An addressing mode where the instruction explicitly contains the address of the data.
Indirect Addressing: An addressing mode where the address of the data is held in a register.
Indexed Addressing: An addressing mode that combines an index register's contents with an offset to calculate the actual address.
Mnemonic Codes: Symbolic instruction codes used in assembly languages to represent machine instructions.
Compiler: A program that translates source code written in a high-level language into machine language so it can be executed by a computer.
Interpreter: A program that directly executes instructions written in a high-level programming language without requiring them to be compiled into machine language first.

Previous Year Solved Question Paper

1. Explain Von Neumann Architecture[Anna University BE 2014]

ANS: Von Neumann architecture forms the core of most digital computer systems and is named after John von Neumann, a mathematician and physicist who contributed to its development in the 1940s. This architecture is based on the concept that data and programs are stored in the computer's memory, making them as accessible as data. This design contrasts with systems where instructions are hard-coded into logic circuits.

The Von Neumann architecture consists of four main components that are interconnected by a system bus:

Memory: Stores both data and instructions in a single read/write memory. This memory can be accessed using addressable locations specified in instructions.
Arithmetic Logic Unit (ALU): Responsible for carrying out all arithmetic and logical operations. The ALU uses operands and code that tells it which operations to perform.
Control Unit (CU): Extracts instructions from memory and decodes and executes them, calling on the ALU when necessary. It controls the flow of data within the computer.
Input/Output (I/O) Devices: These include devices like keyboards, mice, displays, and printers, which are connected to the computer through interfaces that are controlled by the I/O controller.

Operation Structure

In Von Neumann architecture, the CPU operates in a series of steps called the fetch-decode-execute cycle:

Fetch- The control unit retrieves an instruction from memory. The address of this instruction is determined by the program counter, which keeps track of where in the program the computer is operating.
Decode- Once fetched, the instruction is decoded by the control unit. The decoding process involves breaking down the instruction into parts that have operational meaning.
Execute- After decoding, the execute phase begins. This involves the ALU performing arithmetic or logical operations, or it could involve adjusting the program counter to a new value, loading data from memory, or writing data back to memory.

Operand Structures

Operands are the values with which the CPU performs operations. These can be constants (immediate values) or addresses pointing to memory locations. In Von Neumann architecture, operands can be accessed directly from the instruction or read from memory, depending on the instruction type.

Previous Year Unsolved Question Paper

1. Write the advantages and disadvantages of Von Neumann Architecture? [IGNOU MCA 2023]

Exercise

Exercise 1 – Multiple Choice Questions

1. Who is considered the primary developer of the Von Neumann architecture?
   A) Alan Turing
   B) John von Neumann
   C) Charles Babbage
   D) Tim Berners-Lee

2. Which component of the Von Neumann architecture is responsible for carrying out arithmetic and logical operations?
   A) Memory
   B) Arithmetic Logic Unit (ALU)
   C) Control Unit (CU)
   D) Input/Output Devices

3. In the fetch-decode-execute cycle, what is the first step the CPU performs?
   A) Decode
   B) Fetch
   C) Execute
   D) Store

4. What type of memory addressing involves using a register to point to the memory address?
   A) Direct Addressing
   B) Indirect Addressing
   C) Indexed Addressing
   D) Immediate Addressing

5. Which language uses mnemonic codes for operation instructions?

A) Machine Language

B) High-Level Language

C) Assembly Language

D) Markup Language

Exercise 2 – True/False

1. The Von Neumann architecture stores data and instructions in separate memories.
2. Assembly language is easier to learn than high-level languages.
3. The ALU in the Von Neumann architecture is responsible for executing instructions.
4. Mnemonic codes in assembly language make the code more readable for humans.
5. High-level programming languages are generally more portable than assembly languages.

Exercise 3 – Fill in the blanks

1. The control unit retrieves an instruction from memory during the ______ phase.
2. In the Von Neumann architecture, both data and ______ are stored in the same memory.
3. ______ addressing uses an index register combined with a constant to calculate the address.
4. Assembly language is specific to a computer's ______.
5. The mnemonic code 'ADD' in assembly language stands for ______.

Exercise 4- Assertion – Reason

1. **Assertion:** Assembly language is hardware-specific.

Reason: Assembly language provides detailed control over hardware resources.

Options:

A. Both Assertion and Reason are true, and Reason is the correct explanation for Assertion.

B. Both Assertion and Reason are true, but Reason is not the correct explanation for Assertion.

C. Assertion is true, but Reason is false.

D. Both Assertion and Reason are false.

Exercise 12- Small Answers

1. What is the Von Neumann bottleneck?

2. Explain the fetch-decode-execute cycle in the Von Neumann architecture.

3. What is the role of the ALU in a CPU?

4. Describe the concept of indirect addressing.

5. How do high-level languages differ from assembly languages?

Exercise 13- Long Answers

1. Discuss the key components of the Von Neumann architecture and their functions.

2. Explain how the fetch-decode-execute cycle works in the Von Neumann architecture, including the role of the program counter.

Answer

Exercise 1- 1) B , 2) B , 3) B , 4) B , 5) C
Exercise 2- 1) False , 2) False, 3) False , 4) True , 5) True
Exercise 3- 1) fetch , 2) programs , 3) Indexed , 4) architecture , 5) add
Exercise 4- 1) A
Exercise 5- 1)The Von Neumann bottleneck refers to the limitation in computer systems where the shared bus between the CPU and memory for data and instructions creates a bottleneck, leading to operational delays.

2) The fetch-decode-execute cycle is the fundamental operation cycle of the CPU. It involves fetching an instruction from memory, decoding it to understand what action is required, and then executing the instruction by performing the specified operation.

3)The Arithmetic Logic Unit (ALU) is responsible for performing arithmetic operations (such as addition and subtraction) and logical operations (such as comparisons) within the CPU.

4)Indirect addressing is a memory addressing mode where the address of the data is held in a register or a set of registers, rather than being directly specified in the instruction.

5)High-level languages provide greater abstraction from hardware, use more readable syntax similar to human language, and are generally portable across different platforms. Assembly languages provide low-level control, use mnemonic codes for instructions, and are hardware-specific.

Chapter-7
TEST PAPER
Introduction to Computers

Time Duration: 30 Minutes **Maximum Marks: 25**

General Instructions:

1. The question paper consists of questions and is divided into three sections, A, B and C.
2. All questions are compulsory.
3. Section A comprises Fill in the blanks and one word of one mark each.
4. Section B comprises question numbers 1 to 5. These are Short Question carrying two marks each.
5. Section C comprises question numbers 1. These are Long Question carrying five marks each.

SECTION-A

Fill in the blanks- **(1 X 5 = 5 marks)**

1. The Von Neumann architecture uses a single ______ for both data and instructions.
2. In the fetch-decode-execute cycle, the ______ phase involves interpreting the instruction to determine the required action.
3. ______ addressing mode uses an index register to calculate the memory address.
4. Assembly language is often used for ______ programming due to its close interaction with hardware.
5. High-level languages provide greater ______ from the hardware compared to assembly languages.

One word- **(1 X 5 = 5 marks)**

1. What is the fundamental operational cycle of the CPU?
2. Which unit in the CPU is responsible for arithmetic and logical operations?
3. What is the term for symbolic codes used in assembly language?
4. What do you call the type of programming language that is highly abstracted from the hardware?
5. What is the method of protecting data by converting it into a secure format?

SECTION-B

Short Question- **(2 X 5 = 10 marks)**

1. What is the role of the program counter in the CPU?
2. How does indirect addressing differ from direct addressing?
3. Explain the concept of pipelining in CPU architecture.l
4. What are the primary advantages of using high-level programming languages?
5. Describe the function of the Control Unit (CU) in the Von Neumann architecture.

SECTION-C

Long Question- . **(5 marks)**

1. Discuss the differences between assembly language and high-level programming languages in terms of abstraction, control, and usage scenarios. Provide examples of when each type might be preferred.

ONLINE RESOURCES

Chapter 7 Practice Paper
Link: https://forms.gle/orE3LSjoGbAJGgpQ6
QR Code:

Chapter 7 Video Content
Link: https://youtu.be/zXUbL2Scg6g?si=MSN_xMAAitnvA9t1
QR Code:

Chapter 7 Practice Paper
Link https://forms.gle/orE3LSjoGbAJGgpQ6
QR Code

Chapter 7 Video Content
Link:https://youtu.be/zXUbL2Scg6g?si=MSN_xMAAitnvA9t1
QR Code

Chapter 8: Introduction to Programming

In this chapter you will learn about:

Basic Programming Concepts
Programming Paradigms
Introduction to a High-Level Programming Language

Programming is the process of creating a set of instructions that tell a computer how to perform a task. Programming can be used to automate, collect, manage, calculate, and analyze the processing of data and information accurately.

7.1 Basic Programming Concepts

7.1.1 Variables

Variables are the basic units of storage in a program. They are used to hold data that may change during the course of program execution. A variable has a name, a type, and a value.

Example in Python:

```
x = 5
name = "Alice"
```

here x,name are considered as variable.

7.1.2 Data Types

Data types specify the different sizes and values that can be stored in the variable. Common data types include integers, floating-point numbers, characters, strings, and booleans.

Example in Java:

```
int age = 30;
double price = 19.99;
char grade = 'A';
String username = "user123";
boolean isOnline = true;
```

7.1.3 Control Structures

Control statements are fundamental elements in programming that direct the flow of execution of programs. They allow the program to make decisions, repeat operations, and jump between points in the code. There are three main categories of control statements: conditional statements, looping statements, and jump statements. They include decision-making structures (if-else, switch), loops (for, while, do-while), and jump statements (break, continue, return).These control statements are integral to writing efficient, readable, and maintainable code in any programming language. They help to handle different scenarios in program logic, manage repetitive tasks efficiently, and control the program's execution flow based on specific conditions.

Conditional Statements

Conditional statements evaluate a condition and direct the program flow based on whether the condition is true or false. These are critical for decision-making within the code.

A. if Statement

The if statement executes a block of code only if a specified condition is true.

Example in Python:

```
age = 20if age >= 18:
print("You are an adult.")
```

B. if-else Statement

The if-else statement provides an alternative set of instructions if the if condition is false.

Example in Java:

```
int score = 75;if (score >= 80) {
  System.out.println("High Pass");
} else {
  System.out.println("Pass");
}
```

C. else if Ladder

Used for multiple conditions that need to be differentiated.

Example in C#:

```
int number = 0;if (number > 0) {
  Console.WriteLine("Positive");
} else if (number < 0) {
```

```
  Console.WriteLine("Negative");
} else {
  Console.WriteLine("Zero");
}
```

D. switch Statement

The switch statement allows a variable to be tested for equality against a list of values.

Example in C++:

```
char grade = 'B';switch (grade) {
  case 'A':
    cout << "Excellent!";
    break;
  case 'B':
  case 'C':
    cout << "Well done";
    break;
  default:
    cout << "Invalid grade";
}
```

Looping Statements

Looping statements allow a set of instructions to be executed repeatedly based on a condition. These are used to perform repetitive tasks without redundant code.

A. for Loop

Executes a block of code a specific number of times.

Example in Python:

```
for i in range(5):
print(i)
```

B. while Loop

Repeats a block of code as long as a specified condition is true.

Example in Java:

```
int i = 0;while (i < 5) {
   System.out.println(i);
   i++;
}
```

C. do-while Loop

Similar to the while loop, but it guarantees to execute the loop body at least once.

Example in C:

```
int i = 0;do {
   printf("%d\n", i);
   i++;
} while (i < 5);
```

Jump Statements

Jump statements alter the flow by transferring control to another part of the program.

A. break Statement

Terminates the loop or switch statement and transfers execution to the statement immediately following the loop or switch.

Example in C++:

```
for (int i = 0; i < 10; i++) {
   if (i == 5) {
      break;
   }
   count << i << " ";
}
```

B. continue Statement

Causes the loop to skip the remainder of its body and immediately retest its condition prior to reiterating.

Example in Python:

```
for i in range(10):
   if i % 2 == 0:
      continue
```

```
print(i)
```

C. return Statement

Exits from the current function and returns a value from that function.

Example in Java:

```
int doubleValue(int num) {
   return num * 2;
}
```

7.2 Programming Paradigms

7.2.1 Procedural Programming

Procedural programming is based on the concept of procedure calls. Procedures, also known as routines, subroutines, or functions, organize the program into a set of sequential steps.

Example using C (a procedural language):

```
void greet() {
   printf("Hello, World!");
}
int main() {
   greet();
   return 0;
}
```

7.2.2 Object-Oriented Programming (OOP)

OOP is based on the concept of objects, which can contain data, in the form of fields (often known as attributes or properties), and code, in the form of procedures (often known as methods).

Example in Java:

```
public class Car {
   private String color;

   public Car(String color) {
      this.color = color;
   }
```

```
    public void drive() {
        System.out.println("The " + color + " car drives away.");
    }
}
public class Main {
    public static void main(String[] args) {
        Car myCar = new Car("red");
        myCar.drive();
    }
}
```

7.2.3 Functional Programming

Functional programming treats computation as the evaluation of mathematical functions and avoids changing-state and mutable data.

Example in Python:

```
def add(a, b):
    return a + b

result = add(5, 3)print(result)
```

Outputs: 8

7.3 Introduction to a High-Level Programming Language

7.3.1 Python

Python is a high-level, interpreted programming language known for its simplicity and readability, making it one of the most popular languages for beginners and experts alike. Designed by Guido van Rossum and first released in 1991, Python's design philosophy emphasizes code readability with its notable use of significant whitespace. Its language constructs and object-oriented approach aim to help programmers write clear, logical code for small and large-scale projects.

Python supports multiple programming paradigms, including procedural, object-oriented, and functional programming. It features a dynamic type system and automatic memory management, which contribute to its ease of use and maintenance. Moreover, Python has a comprehensive standard library that provides tools suited to many tasks, and its modularity enables programs to be scaled.

The language is widely used in diverse fields such as web development, data analysis, artificial intelligence, scientific computing, and more. Python's vast ecosystem of frameworks and libraries like Flask, Django, NumPy, Pandas, and TensorFlow extend its functionality to web applications, data manipulation, and machine learning. This versatility, coupled with the language's ease of learning, has contributed significantly to its widespread adoption in the tech industry and academia.

Basic Python Program:

```
print("Hello, World!")

name = input("What is your name? ")print("Hello, " + name + "!")
```

7.3.2 Java

Java is a powerful, high-level programming language developed by Sun Microsystems in 1995 and now maintained by Oracle Corporation. It is widely recognized for its philosophy of "Write Once, Run Anywhere" (WORA), meaning that Java code, once compiled into bytecode, can run on any device equipped with a Java Virtual Machine (JVM). This portability makes Java a preferred choice for developing platform-independent applications, including web, mobile, and enterprise applications.

Java is an object-oriented language, emphasizing reusable software components and modularity. This approach allows developers to create modular programs and reusable code, enhancing code readability and maintainability. Java also offers robust security features, automatic memory management through garbage collection, and exception handling capabilities, which contribute to reducing error-prone code and improving application reliability.

Due to its versatility and scalability, Java is used in a variety of computing platforms from embedded devices and mobile phones to enterprise servers and supercomputers. Popular frameworks like Spring and Hibernate facilitate enterprise solutions development, while libraries such as JavaFX support desktop applications with graphical user interfaces. Java's extensive API, powerful development tools like Eclipse and IntelliJ IDEA, and vast developer community make it an enduring choice for developers around the world.

Basic Java Program:

```
public class HelloWorld {
   public static void main(String[] args) {
      System.out.println("Hello, World!");
   }
}
```

7.3.3 C

C is a powerful general-purpose programming language. It is fast, portable, and available on all platforms.The C programming language, developed by Dennis Ritchie in the early 1970s at Bell Labs, is a foundational language in the field of software development. It was originally designed for system programming, particularly for writing operating systems, and has influenced many other languages, including C++, Java, and Python. C is known for its efficiency and control, as it provides low-level access to memory and processes similar to assembly language but with the added benefits of high-level language features.

C's syntax and structured approach make it an ideal choice for developing firmware or portable applications. It operates close to the hardware, offering a powerful mix of hardware accessibility and programming flexibility that remains unmatched by most high-level languages. C's influence is evident in the widespread use of its syntax and style in subsequent programming languages.

Despite its steep learning curve, C continues to be widely used today, particularly in applications requiring optimal performance and memory efficiency. It is integral in the development of modern operating systems, embedded systems, and real-time computational systems. The language's direct manipulation of hardware resources continues to make it a crucial tool for programmers working in system-level development.

Basic C Program:

```
=#include <stdio.h>
int main() {
   printf("Hello, World!\n");
   return 0;
}
```

Summary

Programming Basics involves writing instructions for computers to automate tasks. Key concepts include variables, data types, and control structures.

Variables are named storage locations in memory for holding data that can change during program execution.

Data Types are define the type and size of data a variable can hold, including integers, floating-point numbers, characters, strings, and booleans.

Control Structures are direct the flow of a program's execution and include conditional statements, looping statements, and jump statements.

Procedural Programming uses functions to execute code sequentially.
Object-Oriented Programming (OOP) centers around objects that contain data and methods; useful for modeling real-world scenarios.
Functional Programming focuses on mathematical functions and avoids mutable data, offering a declarative approach to problem-solving.

Glossary

Variable: A memory location with a name and type, used to store data.
Data Type: Specifies the kind of data a variable can hold, such as integer or string.
Conditional Statements: Code structures that perform different actions based on whether a condition is true or false.
Looping Statements: Execute a sequence of instructions repeatedly as long as a condition is met.
Jump Statements: Control the flow by transferring execution to another part of the program.
Function: A block of organized, reusable code that performs a single action.
Object: A data structure containing data (fields) and methods (functions) to manipulate that data.
Class: A blueprint for creating objects.
Method: A function defined within a class that operates on instances of that class.
Interpreter: A program that executes instructions written in a programming language directly, translating them line-by-line.

Previous Year Ssolved Question Paper

1. Write a C program to print all prime numbers between 2000 and 5000 ?[Anna University B.Tech 2014]

ANS:

```
#include <stdio.h>
#include <stdbool.h>

// Function to check if a number is prime
bool isPrime(int num) {
    if (num <= 1) return false;
    for (int i = 2; i * i <= num; i++) {
        if (num % i == 0) return false;
    }
    return true;
}

int main() {
    printf("Prime numbers between 2000 and 5000 are:\n");

    for (int i = 2000; i <= 5000; i++) {
        if (isPrime(i)) {
            printf("%d ", i);
        }
    }

    printf("\n");
    return 0;
}
```

2. What is the static variable? When should it be used?List out the rules to be followed in forming an identifier?[Anna University B.Tech 2015]

ANS: A static variable in C is a variable that retains its value between function calls. It is initialized only once and exists for the lifetime of the program. Static variables can be used within functions, making their scope local to the function, but their lifetime extends until the program ends. They can also be used at the file level to restrict access to the variable to the file in which it is declared.

When to Use Static Variables

Persistent State: When you need a variable to retain its value between function calls, such as counters or state variables.

Limited Scope: When you want a variable to be accessible only within a particular function or file, avoiding global variables.

Memory Efficiency: When you want to limit the memory allocation to a variable to only once, reducing overhead.

Rules for Forming an Identifier in C

Identifiers are names given to various programming elements such as variables, functions, arrays, etc. Here are the rules for forming an identifier:

Alphabetic and Digits: Identifiers can consist of alphabets (both uppercase and lowercase), digits (0-9), and underscores (_).

Cannot Start with a Digit: Identifiers must begin with a letter (a-z, A-Z) or an underscore (_), but not with a digit.

No Special Characters: Identifiers cannot contain special characters like @, #, $, %, etc.

Case Sensitivity: Identifiers are case-sensitive, meaning Variable and variable are considered different identifiers.

Keywords Restriction: Identifiers cannot be the same as C keywords (e.g., int, return, if).

Length: There is no explicit limit to the length of an identifier, but it is advisable to keep them within a reasonable length for readability and maintainability.

Whitespace: Identifiers cannot contain whitespace characters (spaces, tabs).

Previous Year Unsolved Question Paper

1. What is function overriding ? With the help of program, illustrate the concept of function overloading. ?[IGNOU BCA 2023]
2. What is inheritance ? Explain three different types of inheritance.[IGNOU BCA 2023]

Exercise

Exercise 1 – Multiple Choice Questions

1. Which of the following is a variable in Python?
   A) var x = 5;
   B) x = 5
   C) let x = 5;
   D) x := 5

2. Which data type is used to store a character in Java?
   A) char
   B) String
   C) int
   D) bool

3. What type of control structure is used for decision-making?
   A) Looping statements
   B) Conditional statements
   C) Jump statements
   D) Sequential statements

4. Which looping statement guarantees that the loop body will execute at least once?
   A) for loop
   B) while loop
   C) do-while loop
   D) foreach loop

5. What is the primary feature of object-oriented programming?
   A) Functions
   B) Loops
   C) Objects and Classes
   D) Variables

Exercise 2 – True/False

1. In Python, `x = 5` declares a variable x with the value 5.
2. The `while` loop in Java executes a block of code as long as a specified condition is false.
3. Java is an object-oriented programming language.
4. In C programming, `printf` is used to get input from the user.
5. A function in Python is defined using the keyword `func`.

Exercise 3 – Fill in the blanks

1. In Python, a variable can be declared using the syntax x= ______.
2. The `if-else` statement in Java allows for ______ making.
3. A `for` loop is used to execute a block of code a specific number of ______.
4. In Java, a ______ is used to create objects.
5. Functional programming treats computation as the evaluation of mathematical ______.

Exercise 4- Read the questions given below and find the appropriate word in the grid provided.

A	L	M	J	A	V	A
B	C	N	I	L	O	A
S	T	R	I	N	G	M
O	U	T	P	U	T	O

L	P	G	U	I	L	F
P	C	L	A	S	S	B
P	R	O	G	R	A	M

Exercise 5- Small Answers

1. What is the purpose of a variable in programming?
2. Explain the difference between the `while` loop and the `do-while` loop.
3. What is the significance of the `return` statement in a function?
4. How does Python handle code blocks differently from other languages like C or Java?
5. What is the primary characteristic of object-oriented programming?

Exercise 6- Long Answers

1. Explain the concept of control structures in programming and describe the different types of control structures with examples.
2. Discuss the key differences between procedural programming, object-oriented programming (OOP), and functional programming with examples.

Answers

Exercise 1- 1) B , 2) B , 3) A , 4) C , 5) C
Exercise 2- 1) True , 2) False , 3) True , 4) False , 5) False
Exercise 3- 1) 5 , 2) decision , 3) times , 4) class , 5) function-s
Exercise 4-

A	L	M	J	A	V	A
B	C	N	I	L	O	A
S	T	R	I	N	G	M
O	U	T	P	U	T	O
L	P	G	U	I	L	F
P	C	L	A	S	S	B
P	R	O	G	R	A	M

Exercise 5- 1) A variable is used to store data that may change during the execution of a program.
2) The `while` loop checks the condition before executing the loop body, whereas the `do-while` loop executes the loop body at least once before checking the condition.

3)The `return` statement exits the current function and optionally returns a value to the caller.

4)Python uses indentation to define code blocks, whereas languages like C or Java use curly braces `{}`.

5)Object-oriented programming is characterized by the use of objects and classes to model real-world scenarios, encapsulating data and behavior.

Chapter-8
TEST PAPER
Introduction to Computers

Time Duration: 30 Minutes **Maximum Marks: 25**

General Instructions:

1. The question paper consists of questions and is divided into three sections, A, B and C.
2. All questions are compulsory.
3. Section A comprises Fill in the blanks and one word of one mark each.
4. Section B comprises question numbers 1 to 5. These are Short Question carrying two marks each.
5. Section D comprises question numbers 1. These are Long Questio carrying five marks each.

SECTION-A

Fill in the blanks- **(1 X 5 = 5 marks)**

1. In Python, a ______ is used to define a function.
2. The ______ keyword in Java is used to create an instance of a class.
3. In procedural programming, the code is organized into ______.
4. In C, the ______ function is used to print text to the console.
5. In object-oriented programming, ______ allows a subclass to inherit properties and methods from a superclass.

One word- **(1 X 5 = 5 marks)**

1. What is the smallest unit of storage in a program?
2. Which programming paradigm focuses on objects containing data and methods?
3. Which keyword is used in Python to create a loop that iterates over a sequence?
4. What is the process of converting a high-level language into machine code called?
5. Which Java statement is used to handle exceptions?

SECTION-B

Short Question- **(2 X 5 = 10 marks)**

1. What is the role of a variable in programming?
2. Describe the purpose of the `if-else` statement in programming.
3. How does the `for` loop differ from the `while` loop in programming?
4. Explain the concept of encapsulation in object-oriented programming.
5. What are the advantages of using high-level programming languages over low-level languages?

SECTION-C

Long Question- . **(5 marks)**

1. Discuss the key features of object-oriented programming (OOP) and provide examples of how OOP principles are applied in a Java program.

ONLINE RESOURCES

Chapter 8 Practice Paper
Link
https://forms.gle/2xeuio3xs8pBueds5
QR Code

Chapter 8 Video Content
Link
https://youtu.be/rHMkD_WG6Lk?si=9ld-s4JCB5cgjX3e
QR Code

Chapter 9: Introduction to Database Systems

In this chapter you will learn about :

Basics of Databases and Database Management Systems Relational Database Concepts
Introduction to SQL

9.1 Basics of Databases and Database Management Systems

Databases are the backbone of modern information systems, playing a pivotal role in storing, organizing, and managing data efficiently. This section provides a fundamental understanding of databases, their significance, and the distinction between data and information.
Information systems are complex networks of hardware, software, data, and people that work together to collect, process, store, and disseminate information for various purposes within an organization. Databases play a pivotal role in information systems, serving as their foundational backbone. Let's delve into the intricate details of how databases contribute to the functionality of information systems:

Efficiency in Data Storage: Databases efficiently store vast amounts of data in a structured and organized manner. This ensures that data is readily accessible when needed, eliminating the need for paper-based or scattered electronic records.
Data Integration: Information systems often gather data from multiple sources, such as sales, inventory, customer records, and more. Databases allow for the integration of this diverse data into a unified and coherent structure.
Data Retrieval and Reporting: Databases provide powerful querying capabilities, allowing users to retrieve specific data or generate complex reports. This is crucial for decision-making processes, as it enables users to extract relevant information from large datasets.
Data Security: Information systems deal with sensitive and critical data. Databases include security features such as user authentication, access controls, and encryption to protect data from unauthorized access and ensure data integrity.
Data Consistency: Databases enforce data consistency by maintaining relationships between different data elements. This ensures that data remains accurate and coherent throughout the system, even when multiple users access it simultaneously.

Redundancy Reduction: Redundancy in data storage can lead to inconsistencies and increased storage costs. Databases are designed to minimize data redundancy by storing each piece of information in one location, thus reducing the risk of conflicting data.

Data Scalability: As organizations grow, their data needs increase. Databases are scalable, allowing organizations to expand their data storage and processing capabilities seamlessly, ensuring the information system can accommodate future growth.

Data Recovery and Backup: Databases include mechanisms for data backup and recovery. This is crucial for disaster recovery and ensuring that data is not lost due to hardware failures, errors, or other unforeseen events.

Data Analysis and Business Intelligence: Databases serve as the foundation for data analysis and business intelligence tools. They enable organizations to derive insights, make data-driven decisions, and gain a competitive edge in the market.

Streamlined Workflows: Information systems leverage databases to automate and streamline workflows. This includes processes such as order processing, inventory management, and customer relationship management.

Decision Support: Databases facilitate decision support systems by providing historical and real-time data, enabling organizations to make informed decisions based on accurate and up-to-date information.

Characteristics of a Database

Databases are critical components of modern information systems, offering a structured and efficient way to store, manage, and retrieve data. Understanding the characteristics of a database is essential for effective data management and utilization. Here are the key characteristics in detail:

Data Integrity: Data integrity refers to the accuracy and consistency of data stored in the database. It ensures that data is reliable and trustworthy.

Data Consistency: Data consistency ensures that data remains uniform and coherent across the database, even when multiple users or applications access it simultaneously.

Data Security: Data security safeguards data from unauthorized access, modification, or disclosure. It protects sensitive information from breaches and unauthorized use.

Data Accessibility: Data accessibility ensures that authorized users can access data when needed. It involves making data available while maintaining security and privacy.

Data Scalability: Scalability refers to the database's ability to handle growing volumes of data and increasing user demands without significant performance degradation.

Data Recovery and Backup: Data recovery and backup features ensure that data can be restored in case of hardware failures, data corruption, or accidental deletions.
Data Redundancy Reduction: Redundancy reduction minimizes the duplication of data within the database. It helps maintain data consistency and reduces storage costs.
Transaction Management: Transaction management ensures that database operations (e.g., insert, update, delete) are carried out reliably and maintain data consistency.
Data Backup and Recovery: Data backup and recovery mechanisms provide safeguards against data loss due to hardware failures, errors, or unforeseen events.

Data Modelling and Schema: Data modelling involves creating a logical representation of the database's structure using schema design, defining tables, relationships, and constraints.

Database Management System

In a Database Management System (DBMS), keys play a fundamental role in organizing and identifying data within a database. They are essential for maintaining data integrity, ensuring data uniqueness, and establishing relationships between tables. Here's an in-depth look at keys in DBMS:

Primary Key (PK):

A primary key is a unique identifier for each record (row) in a table.
It ensures data integrity by guaranteeing that each record has a distinct and non-null identifier.
A table can have only one primary key, and it is typically implemented as an indexed column.

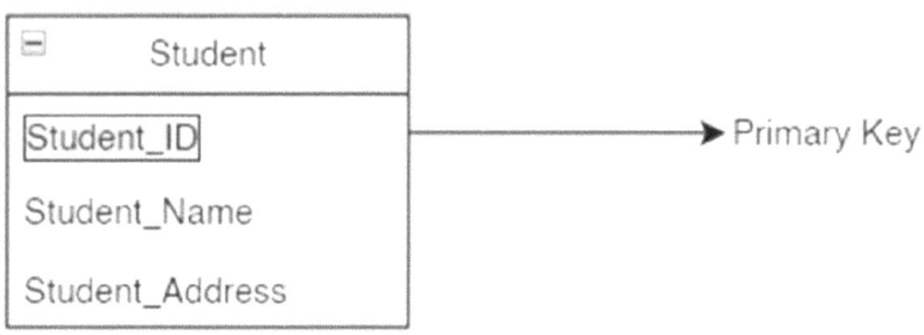

Primary keys are used as references (foreign keys) in other tables to establish relationships between tables.

Candidate Key:

A candidate key is a set of one or more columns that could potentially serve as the primary key of a table.
Like the primary key, candidate keys must ensure uniqueness and integrity.

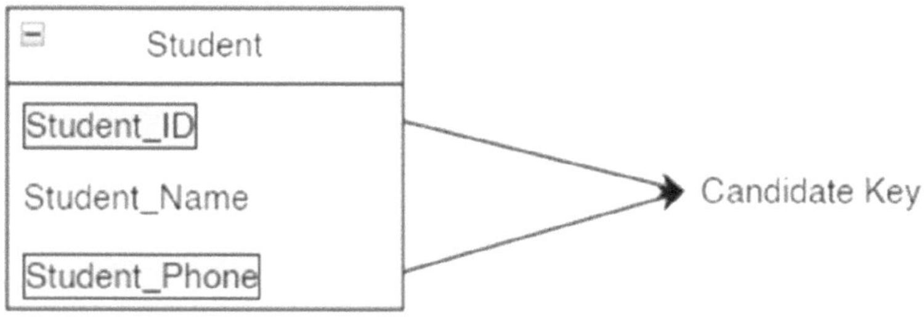

When there are multiple candidate keys, one is chosen as the primary key, and the others become alternate keys.

Alternate Key:

An alternate key is a candidate key that is not selected as the primary key.
While it is not the primary means of identifying records, it can still be used for unique identification.
Alternate keys can provide additional options for querying and indexing data.

Composite Key:

A composite key consists of two or more columns used together as a single key.
It is employed when no single column can uniquely identify records, but a combination of columns can.
Composite keys are often used in junction tables for many-to-many relationships.

Foreign Key (FK):

A foreign key is a column or a set of columns in one table that refers to the primary key of another table.
It establishes relationships between tables, enforcing referential integrity.
Foreign keys ensure that values in the referencing table (child table) correspond to values in the referenced table (parent table).
They help maintain data consistency and enforce data relationships.

Super Key:

A super key is a set of one or more columns that can uniquely identify a record within a table.
It can include more columns than required for a minimal identifier.
A super key is a broader concept than a candidate key because it can contain additional attributes.

Natural Key vs. Surrogate Key:

A natural key is a key composed of existing, meaningful data attributes (e.g., a person's social security number).

A surrogate key is a system-generated key, often an auto-incremented number, used as a primary key to ensure uniqueness. It has no inherent meaning.

Unique Key:

A unique key is similar to a primary key in that it enforces uniqueness but may allow null values.
Unlike a primary key, a table can have multiple unique keys.
Unique keys are often used when you need to ensure data integrity without enforcing a primary key constraint.

9.2 Relational Database Concepts

Relational Algebra in Database Management Systems (DBMS) is a mathematical system used for manipulating and querying data stored in relational databases. It provides a formal and theoretical framework for performing operations on the data within a relational database. The key operations in relational algebra are:

Selection (σ): This operation is used to retrieve rows from a relation (table) that satisfy a specific condition. It is akin to the SQL WHERE clause. For example, selecting all employees with a salary greater than $50,000 would be expressed as σ (salary > 50000) (Employees).

Projection (π): Projection is used to select specific columns from a relation while discarding others. It is similar to the SQL SELECT statement but focuses on columns rather than rows. For instance, projecting only the "name" and "age" columns from the "Persons" relation would be written as π(name, age)(Persons).

Union (∪): The union operation combines two relations with the same schema (attributes) to create a new relation that contains all unique rows from both input relations. For example, if we have two sets of students, A and B, the union of these sets would include all distinct students from both sets.

Intersection (∩): The intersection operation combines two relations to create a new relation containing only the rows that appear in both input relations. It is like finding common elements between two sets.

Difference (-): The difference operation is used to find the rows that are unique to one relation and do not appear in another. For example, if we have two sets of students, A and B, the difference between A and B would include students who are in set A but not in set B.

Cartesian Product (×): The Cartesian product combines every row from the first relation with every row from the second relation, resulting in a new relation with a combination of rows from both relations. It generates all possible pairs of rows from the input relations.

Join (⋈): Join operations are used to combine rows from two or more relations based on a related column (attribute). Different types of join include inner join, outer join (left, right, and full outer joins), and natural join. They are similar to SQL join operations.

Rename(ρ): The rename operation is used to rename the output relation. It is denoted by rho (ρ).
Example: We can use the rename operator to rename STUDENT relation to STUDENT1.
Relational algebra serves as the foundation for query languages like SQL and helps database systems understand and process user queries. It provides a precise and systematic way of expressing operations on relational data, facilitating efficient data retrieval and manipulation in relational database management systems.

Cartesian Product:

The Cartesian product is an operation that combines all rows from one table with all rows from another table to produce a result set. It's also known as the cross product or simply "times."

For two tables, A and B, the Cartesian product, denoted as A × B, generates a new table where each row from table A is paired with every row from table B. The resulting table contains (number of rows in A) × (number of rows in B) rows.

Example:

Let's illustrate the Cartesian product with a simple example. Consider two tables, "Customers" and "Products," as follows:

Customers Table:

CustomerID	CustomerName
1	Alice
2	Bob

Products Table:

ProductID	ProductName
101	Laptop
102	Smartphone

Now, let's find the Cartesian product of these two tables (Customers × Products):

Resulting Table (Customers × Products):

CustomerID	CustomerName	ProductID	ProductName
1	Alice	101	Laptop
1	Alice	102	Smartphone
2	Bob	101	Laptop
2	Bob	102	Smartphone

In the resulting table, each row from the "Customers" table is paired with every row from the "Products" table, creating all possible combinations.

Division Operator:

The division operator, denoted as ÷, is a relational algebra operation used to retrieve records from one table that are related to all records in another table without any remaining related records. In other words, it finds those tuples in a relation (table) that are associated with all the values in another relation.

The division operation is typically used when dealing with many-to-many relationships in a database. It helps identify entities that have relationships with all specified related entities.

Example of Division Operator:

Let's consider two tables: "Students" and "Courses."

Students Table:

Student_ID	Student_Name
1	Alice
2	Bob
3	Carol

Courses Table:

Course_ID	Course_Name
101	Math
102	Physics

Suppose we want to find students who have taken all the courses in the "Courses" table. The result of the division operation will be an empty set because no student has taken all the courses.

Set Difference Operator:

The set difference operator, denoted as "-", is used to retrieve records from one table that do not have matching records in another table. It returns the difference between two sets of records, where the records in one set are not present in the other set.

Example of Set Difference Operator:

Let's consider two tables: "Employees" and "Managers."

Employees Table:

Employee_ID	Employee_Name
1	Alice
2	Bob
3	Carol
4	David

Managers Table:

Manager_ID	Manager_Name
2	Bob
4	David

If we want to find employees who are not managers, we can use the set difference operator. The result will be:

Employee_ID	Employee_Name
1	Alice
3	Carol

These employees are not present in the "Managers" table.

Query optimization:

Query optimization is a crucial component of database management systems (DBMS) that aims to improve the efficiency and performance of database queries. It involves selecting the most efficient execution plan for a given query from a set of possible execution plans. The primary goal of query optimization is to minimize the query's execution time and resource usage while producing the correct and desired results.

The process of query optimization typically involves the following steps:

Parsing and Validation: The first step is parsing and validating the SQL query to ensure its correctness and adherence to the database schema.
Query Rewriting: This step involves transforming the query into an equivalent but more optimized form. Techniques like query rewriting can simplify complex queries and make them more amenable to optimization.
Candidate Plan Generation: The query optimizer generates multiple candidate execution plans, each representing a different way to retrieve the required data. These plans consider various factors, such as the order of table access, join methods, and index usage.
Cost Estimation: The optimizer estimates the cost associated with each candidate execution plan. The cost includes factors like I/O operations, CPU usage, and network communication.
Plan Selection: Based on the cost estimates, the optimizer selects the execution plan with the lowest estimated cost. This plan is considered the optimal plan for executing the query.
Plan Execution: Finally, the selected execution plan is executed to retrieve the query results.

Relationship to Join Operation:
The Cartesian product operation is related to the join operation in that it forms the foundation for certain types of joins. Specifically, the Cartesian product is used as an intermediate step in the calculation of a cross join (also known as a Cartesian join) and certain types of outer joins.

Cross Join (Cartesian Join): A cross join is a join operation that produces the Cartesian product of two tables. In SQL, you can achieve this using the CROSS JOIN keyword. For example, SELECT * FROM Customers CROSS JOIN Products; would produce the same result as the Cartesian product of the two tables shown earlier.

Outer Joins: While the Cartesian product itself is not directly used for inner joins (they generally involve conditions for matching rows), it becomes relevant when performing outer joins. Outer joins involve keeping unmatched rows from one table, and the Cartesian product can be used to determine which rows are unmatched.

9.3 Introduction to SQL

Data Manipulation Language (DML) is a subset of SQL (Structured Query Language) used to interact with and manipulate data stored in a relational database management system (DBMS). DML primarily consists of SQL statements for querying, inserting, updating, and deleting data within database tables. Below are detailed explanations of common DML statements:

SELECT Statement (Data Retrieval):

Purpose: The SELECT statement retrieves data from one or more tables in the database.

```
Syntax: SELECT column1, column2, ...
        FROM table_name
        WHERE condition;
```

Explanation:

SELECT: Specifies the columns to retrieve or use `*` to select all columns.

FROM: Specifies the table(s) from which to retrieve data.

WHERE (optional): Filters rows based on a specified condition.

INSERT Statement (Data Insertion):

Purpose: The INSERT statement adds new records (rows) to a table.

```
Syntax: INSERT INTO table_name (column1, column2, ...)
        VALUES (value1, value2, ...);
```

Explanation:

INSERT INTO: Specifies the target table.

(column1, column2, ...): Lists the columns to insert data into.

VALUE: Provides corresponding values for each column.

UPDATE Statement (Data Modification):

Purpose: The UPDATE statement modifies existing records in a table.

```
Syntax: UPDATE table_name
        SET column1 = value1, column2 = value2, ...
        WHERE condition;
```

Explanation:

UPDATE: Specifies the table to be updated.

SET: Assigns new values to columns.

WHERE (optional): Specifies the rows to be updated based on a condition.

DELETE Statement (Data Deletion):

Purpose: The DELETE statement removes records from a table.

```
Syntax: DELETE FROM table_name
        WHERE condition;
```

Explanation:

DELETE FROM: Specifies the table from which to delete data.

WHERE (optional): Filters rows to be deleted based on a condition.

MERGE Statement (Upsert Operation):

Purpose: The MERGE statement performs an "upsert" operation, which means it inserts a row if it doesn't exist or updates it if it does.

```
Syntax: MERGE INTO target_table AS target
        USING source_table AS source
        ON condition
        WHEN MATCHED THEN
        UPDATE SET column1 = value1, ...
        WHEN NOT MATCHED THEN
         INSERT (column1, column2, ...)
        VALUES (value1, value2, ...);
```

Explanation:

MERGE INTO: Specifies the target table and aliases it as "target."

USING: Specifies the source table and aliases it as "source."

ON: Defines the condition to match records.

WHEN MATCHED and WHEN NOT MATCHED clauses allow for different actions based on whether a match is found or not.

DML statements are essential for manipulating the data stored in a relational database. These statements enable you to query for specific information, insert new data, update existing data, and remove data as needed. Properly constructed DML statements ensure data accuracy, integrity, and consistency within the database.

9.3.1 Procedural DML:

Specifies How: Procedural DMLs are designed to specify not only "what" data operations should be performed but also "how" they should be carried out. They involve detailed step-by-step instructions to achieve a specific data manipulation task.

Precise Control: Programmers using procedural DMLs have precise control over the sequence of operations. They need to specify every detail, including iteration and conditional logic, for achieving the desired outcome.
Complexity: Procedural DMLs tend to be more complex and require a deeper understanding of programming concepts. Developers need to handle data access and control flow explicitly.

Examples: SQL/PSM (SQL/Persistent Stored Modules) and PL/SQL (Procedural Language/SQL) are examples of procedural DMLs used in relational database systems like Oracle and PostgreSQL.

9.3.2 Non-Procedural DML:

Specifies What: Non-procedural DMLs focus solely on "what" data operations should be performed, leaving the "how" to the database management system (DBMS). Instead of specifying a step-by-step procedure, users declare their data requirements.
Higher Abstraction: Non-procedural DMLs provide a higher level of abstraction. Users describe their data needs in a declarative manner without getting into implementation details.
Simplicity: They are often simpler for end-users because they don't need to be concerned with programming logic. Users state what data they want without specifying how to retrieve it.

Examples: SQL (Structured Query Language) is a prime example of a non-procedural DML. Users write SQL queries that declare what data they want from the database, and the DBMS's query optimizer determines the most efficient way to retrieve it.

Summary

Databases store, organize, and manage data efficiently.
Essential for modern information systems.
Enable efficient data retrieval, integration, security, and scalability.
Keys ensure data integrity and relationships.

Glossary

Database: A structured collection of data stored electronically.
DBMS: Software that manages and controls access to a database.
Primary Key: Unique identifier for a record in a table.
Foreign Key: Column(s) in one table that refer to the primary key in another table.

Relational Algebra: Theoretical foundation for querying relational databases.

DML: Data Manipulation Language, used for querying and modifying data.

SQL: Structured Query Language, used for managing and manipulating relational databases.

Procedural DML: Specifies how data operations should be performed.

Non-Procedural DML: Specifies what data operations should be performed without detailing how.

Previous Year Solved Question Paper

1. What is Database ? Explain database development life cycle.[IGNOU CIT 2023]

ANS: A database is an organized collection of data, typically stored and accessed electronically from a computer system. Databases are designed to manage, store, retrieve, and manipulate data efficiently. They are used in various applications, from simple data storage solutions to complex enterprise-level systems.

Database Development Life Cycle (DDLC)

The Database Development Life Cycle (DDLC) is a structured approach used to design, implement, and maintain a database system. It includes several phases:

Requirements Analysis:

Objective: Identify the data needs of the organization or project.

Activities: Gather requirements through interviews, surveys, and document analysis. Define the scope and objectives of the database.

Conceptual Design:

Objective: Create a high-level design of the database independent of the DBMS.

Activities: Develop an Entity-Relationship (ER) diagram to represent the data entities, attributes, and relationships. Ensure the design meets the requirements identified.

Logical Design:

Objective: Transform the conceptual design into a logical model that can be implemented in a specific DBMS.

Activities: Normalize the data model to eliminate redundancy and ensure data integrity. Define tables, columns, keys, and relationships.

Physical Design:

Objective: Convert the logical design into a physical structure that can be implemented and optimized on the chosen DBMS.

Activities: Define the physical storage of the data, including indexing, partitioning, and clustering. Optimize for performance and storage efficiency.

Implementation:

Objective: Create the actual database in the chosen DBMS.

Activities: Write SQL scripts to create tables, indexes, views, and constraints. Populate the database with initial data. Implement security measures.

Testing:

Objective: Ensure the database meets all requirements and functions correctly.

Activities: Perform various tests, including unit testing, integration testing, and performance testing. Identify and fix defects or issues.

Deployment:

Objective: Make the database system available for use in a production environment.

Activities: Migrate the database to the production server. Perform final data loading and setup. Ensure all users have the necessary access and training.

Maintenance:

Objective: Keep the database system running smoothly and efficiently.

Activities: Monitor performance, perform backups, apply updates and patches, and handle user support and troubleshooting. Plan and implement improvements and optimizations as needed.

Previous Year Unsolved Question Paper

1. Differentiate between DBMS and RDBMS. Under what situation is it better to use file base system than database system ?[IGNOU MCA 2023]
2. Differentiate between DBMS and RDBMS. Under what situation is it better to use file base system than database system ?[IGNOU MCA 2023]

Exercise

Exercise 1 – Multiple Choice Questions

1. What is the primary function of a database?
   A) Storing and organizing data
   B) Executing programs
   C) Compiling code
   D) Managing hardware

2. Which of the following is NOT a characteristic of a database?
   A) Data Integrity
   B) Data Consistency
   C) Data Redundancy
   D) Data Scalability

3. A ______ is a unique identifier for each record in a table.
   A) Foreign Key
   B) Primary Key
   C) Composite Key
   D) Alternate Key
   Correct Answer: B

4. Which SQL statement is used to retrieve data from a database?
   A) INSERT
   B) UPDATE
   C) SELECT
   D) DELETE

5. Relational Algebra operation that retrieves rows from a relation based on a condition:
   A) Projection
   B) Selection
   C) Union
   D) Intersection

Exercise 2 – True/False

1. A primary key can have duplicate values.
2. The SELECT statement is used to delete records from a table.
3. Data integrity ensures that data is accurate and consistent.
4. A foreign key refers to the primary key in another table.
5. The UNION operation in relational algebra combines rows from two tables.

Exercise 3 – Fill in the blanks

1. The ______ key ensures that each record in a table is unique.
2. SQL is used to ______ and manipulate data in a database.
3. The ______ operation in relational algebra combines rows from two tables based on a related column.
4. The ______ key in one table refers to the primary key in another table.
5. The ______ operation in relational algebra is used to retrieve specific columns.

Exercise 4 - One- word

1. What is a unique identifier for each record in a table?
2. What SQL statement is used to delete records from a table?
3. What type of key is used to establish relationships between tables?
4. What relational algebra operation retrieves specific columns?
5. What is a system-generated key with no inherent meaning called?

Exercise 5 - Small Answers

1. What is the role of a primary key in a database?
2. Explain the difference between procedural and non-procedural DML.
3. What is a foreign key and why is it important?
4. Describe the projection operation in relational algebra.
5. How does the UNION operation differ from the INTERSECTION operation in relational algebra?

Exercise 6 - Long Answers

1. Describe the various types of data, including structured, unstructured, semi-structured, and provide real-world examples of each type. Explain why understanding these data types is important in data management and database design.

2. Explain the fundamental difference between data and information. Provide examples to illustrate the concept and discuss why this distinction is important in the context of data management and decision-making.

Answer

Exercise 1- 1) A , 2) C , 3) B , 4) C , 5) B
Exercise 2- 1) False , 2) False , 3) True , 4) True , 5) True
Exercise 3- 1) Primary , 2) query , 3) join , 4) foreign , 5) projection
Exercise 4- 1) Primary Key ,
2) DELETE ,
3) Foreign ,
4) Projection ,
5) Surrogate

Exercise 5- 1)A primary key uniquely identifies each record in a table, ensuring data integrity and preventing duplicate records.

2)Procedural DML specifies how data operations should be performed, while non-procedural DML specifies what data operations should be performed without detailing how.

3)A foreign key is a column or set of columns in one table that refers to the primary key in another table. It is important for establishing and enforcing relationships between tables, ensuring referential integrity.

4)The projection operation retrieves specific columns from a relation, discarding the other columns.

5) The UNION operation combines rows from two tables, including all unique rows from both tables. The INTERSECTION operation retrieves only the rows that are common to both tables.

Chapter-9
TEST PAPER
Introduction to Computers

Time Duration: 30 Minutes **Maximum Marks: 25**

General Instructions:

1. The question paper consists of questions and is divided into three sections, A, B and C.
2. All questions are compulsory.
3. Section A comprises Fill in the blanks and True/False of one mark each.
4. Section B comprises question numbers 1 to 5. These are Short Question carrying two marks each.
5. Section C comprises question numbers 1. These are Long Question carrying five marks each.

SECTION-A

Fill in the blanks- **(1 X 5 = 5 marks)**

1. The ______ key in a database ensures that each record has a unique identifier.
2. In SQL, the ______ statement is used to retrieve data from a database.
3. A ______ key is used to establish a relationship between two tables.
4. The ______ operation in relational algebra retrieves specific columns from a table.
5. A ______ key is a combination of two or more columns used together to uniquely identify a record.

True/False- **(1 X 5 = 5 marks)**

1. A primary key can contain null values.
2. The DELETE statement in SQL is used to remove records from a table.
3. A foreign key can reference multiple primary keys in different tables.
4. Data redundancy increases storage costs and the risk of conflicting data.
5. The Cartesian Product operation in relational algebra combines all rows from one table with all rows from another table.

SECTION-B

Short Question- **(2 X 5 = 10 marks)**

1. What is a database and why is it important?
2. Explain the concept of data integrity in a database.
3. What is the role of a DBMS (Database Management System)?
4. Describe the difference between a primary key and a unique key.
5. What is relational algebra and why is it important in databases?

SECTION-C

Long Question- . **(5 marks)**

1. Discuss the role and importance of keys in a Database Management System (DBMS). Explain different types of keys and their functions with examples.

ONLINE RESOURCES

Chapter 9 Practice Paper
Link
https://forms.gle/YssKNB7KdwaJomvB8
QR Code

Chapter 9 Video Content
Link
https://youtu.be/L_KncQggjxE?si=-Q2b-gJX8ckFMWsf
QR Code

Chapter 10: Microsoft Office

In this chapter you will learn about :

Overview of Microsoft Office	MS Word
MS Excel	MS Power Point
MS Outlook	MS Access
MS Teams	

1.1 Overview of Microsoft Office

Microsoft Office is a suite of productivity tools developed by Microsoft, widely used in business, educational, and personal environments to facilitate document creation, data management, communication, and presentation. Initially launched in 1989, Microsoft Office has evolved significantly, integrating more features and applications to meet the growing demands of users across various platforms.

The core components of Microsoft Office include Word, Excel, PowerPoint, and Outlook. Each of these applications serves a specific purpose but is designed to work seamlessly together. **Microsoft Word** is a powerful word processor that allows users to create complex documents with formatted text, images, and advanced page layout options. **Microsoft Excel** is a spreadsheet program known for its robust data analysis tools, including functions, formulas, and pivot tables that help users in detailed data examination and visualization. **Microsoft PowerPoint** is used to create dynamic and visually compelling presentations, essential for professional and educational presentations to convey information effectively.**Microsoft Outlook**, on the other hand, is an all-in-one email, calendar, and task management tool, crucial for personal information management and communication within and outside an organization.Over the years, Microsoft has expanded the Office suite to include other tools like OneNote, a versatile note-taking app; Access, a database management system; and Publisher, a desktop publishing app.

More recently, Microsoft has embraced cloud computing with the introduction of Office 365 (rebranded as Microsoft 365), which offers subscription-based access to Office applications, along with cloud storage on OneDrive and various other cloud-based features.Microsoft Office's integration with Microsoft Teams, a platform that combines workplace chat, meetings, notes, and attachments, has further enhanced its utility in collaborative and remote working environments. This integration ensures that Office remains relevant and continues to be an indispensable tool in the digital workplace, providing comprehensive solutions that support a wide range of productivity tasks.

10.2 MS Word

Microsoft Word is a computer application program written by Microsoft. It is mainly used to design text for presentation.

Our MS Word tutorial includes all topics of MS Word such as save the document, correct error, word count, font size, font style, apply a style, customize a style, page size, page margin, insert header and footer and more.

Microsoft Word is renowned for its user-friendly interface and an extensive set of features that cater to the needs of individuals, businesses, educational institutions, and government organizations. Some key aspects of the software include:

Document Creation: Word allows users to create documents from scratch, whether it's a simple letter, a report, a thesis, or a complex business proposal. Users can start with a blank document or choose from a wide range of pre-designed templates to kickstart their work.
Text Formatting: Word provides a variety of text formatting options, enabling users to control fonts, sizes, styles, colors, and alignment. It also offers tools for creating headings, subheadings, and lists, improving the visual appeal and organization of documents.
Document Editing: Users can easily edit their documents, insert, delete, or move text, and make corrections with the built-in spell check and grammar check tools. The track changes feature is valuable for collaborative editing and reviewing.
Visual Content: Word allows users to embed images, charts, graphs, and shapes into documents, enhancing the visual representation of information. Users can also create tables for structured data presentation.
Document Organization: It offers features like headers, footers, page numbering, and table of contents creation, making it easier to organize and navigate longer documents. Sections and breaks enable different layouts within a single document.
Collaboration: Word supports real-time collaboration, where multiple users can work on a document simultaneously. Comments and markups facilitate communication and feedback among collaborators.
Integration: As part of the Microsoft Office suite, Word seamlessly integrates with other Microsoft applications like Excel, PowerPoint, and Outlook, enabling users to combine various types of content and data.
Cloud Integration: Users can save and access their documents on Microsoft OneDrive or SharePoint, making it possible to work on documents from different devices and share them with others.
Compatibility: Documents created in Word can be saved in various formats, making them accessible to users of other word processing software. Common formats include .docx, .pdf, and .rtf.

10.2.1 History of MS Word

Microsoft Word, a widely used word processing software, has a rich history that spans several decades. Its development can be traced back to the early 1980s when Microsoft embarked on a mission to create a user-friendly word processing application for personal computers.
The journey of Microsoft Word began in 1983 when the first version, known as Multi-Tool Word, was released for the Xenix operating system. However, it was with the release of Word 1.0 for MS-DOS in 1983 that Microsoft gained a foothold in the word processing market.
Over the years, Microsoft Word underwent significant transformations and updates to meet the evolving needs of users. With the release of Word 2.0 in 1985, Microsoft introduced features such as

the ability to bold and italicize text, enhancing the formatting capabilities of the software. Subsequent versions, like Word 3.0 and Word 4.0, continued to refine the user interface and functionality.
The 1990s marked a period of rapid advancement for Microsoft Word. The release of Word 95 introduced the iconic toolbar and menu system, making it more intuitive for users to navigate and access various features. This version also embraced the concept of "What You See Is What You Get" (WYSIWYG) editing, providing a more accurate representation of the final document on the screen.
The late 1990s and early 2000s saw the integration of Microsoft Word into the Microsoft Office suite, which further solidified its place as a comprehensive office productivity tool. Word 2000 brought enhanced collaboration features, allowing multiple users to work on a document simultaneously.
As the digital landscape evolved, so did Microsoft Word. The introduction of Office 2003 brought improved XML support, making it easier to manage and manipulate document content. Subsequent versions, such as Word 2007 and Word 2010, focused on enhancing the user experience with the introduction of the Ribbon interface and increased collaboration capabilities.
The advent of cloud computing and mobile technology influenced the development of Word Online and Word Mobile, enabling users to create and edit documents on the go. Microsoft Word 2013 and Word 2016 continued to refine features, emphasizing collaboration through real-time co-authoring and cloud integration.
In recent years, Microsoft has embraced artificial intelligence (AI) and machine learning to enhance Word's capabilities further. Features like Editor, which provides grammar and writing suggestions, showcase the ongoing commitment to improving the user experience.
Microsoft Word remains a staple in homes, offices, and educational institutions worldwide. Its enduring popularity can be attributed to continuous innovation, adaptability to changing technological landscapes, and a commitment to providing users with powerful yet user-friendly tools for document creation and editing.

10.2.2 Importance of Microsoft Word

Document Creation and Editing: Microsoft Word allows users to create, edit, and format documents of various types, such as letters, reports, essays, and more. It provides a user-friendly interface for easy content creation.
Professional Documentation: It is widely used for creating professional documents, including resumes, business letters, and official reports. Its formatting features enable users to produce polished and well-organized documents.
Spell Check and Grammar Check: Microsoft Word includes built-in spelling and grammar checking tools, helping users create error-free documents. This is vital for maintaining professionalism and clarity.

Document Formatting: Word offers extensive formatting options for text, paragraphs, and pages. Users can customize fonts, styles, margins, and spacing to make documents visually appealing and consistent.

Templates and Styles: It provides a wide range of document templates and styles, saving time and effort in document design. Templates for resumes, newsletters, and more are readily available.

Collaboration: Microsoft Word offers collaborative features, allowing multiple users to edit and comment on the same document simultaneously. This is crucial for teamwork and document review.

Document Organization: Word provides features like tables of contents, headers, and footers for effective document organization. These tools enhance the structure and navigability of documents.

Integration: It seamlessly integrates with other Microsoft Office applications, such as Excel and PowerPoint, for a more comprehensive and cohesive office suite.

Compatibility: Documents created in Microsoft Word can be easily shared and opened by others, making it a universal standard for document sharing and communication.

Research and References: It has tools for managing citations, references, and bibliographies, making it a valuable tool for academic and research-related documents.

Automation and Macros: Advanced users can create custom macros and automate repetitive tasks, increasing efficiency and productivity.

Digital Signatures: Microsoft Word allows for the integration of digital signatures, ensuring document security and authenticity.

Cloud Integration: With Microsoft 365 and OneDrive, documents can be stored in the cloud, making them accessible from anywhere and facilitating real-time collaboration.

Accessibility Features: It includes accessibility tools for creating documents that are inclusive and can be read by individuals with disabilities.

Version Control: Users can track changes and revert to previous versions of a document, which is crucial for document management and collaboration.

10.3 MS Excel

Microsoft Excel is a spreadsheet program that comes bundled with the Microsoft Office suite of business applications. It provides various tools and features to format, organize and calculate data in a spreadsheet format, making it easier to view and analyze the data. Excel uses a grid of cells arranged in rows and columns to store data. Users can input data into these cells and perform calculations on them. By organizing data in this way, data analysts and other users can make sense of large data sets more easily.

10.3.1 Advantages of Using MS Excel

The advantages of using MS Excel are as follows:

Data Storage: MS Excel is widely used in many organizations as a large amount of data is stored in Excel. The user can edit and retrieve the data whenever needed. Hence filtering the data is a quick and easy process.

Data Recovery: Data Recovery is done quickly in Excel. If data is written on paper, it isn't easy to recover and filter it. But it is easy to find and recover the data in Excel Spreadsheet.

Mathematical Calculations: Excel consists of a variety of formulas that are used to perform mathematical calculations. Based on the data and requirements, the formula is modified.

Data Privacy: Data security and privacy is ensured in Excel. The Personal Computer and laptop are secured with a password; hence data is protected.

All data in one place: In earlier days, the records and data were maintained in separate files, which were difficult to take and time-consuming process. In Excel
the data are stored in one Excel file, which is used to analyze the data whenever needed.

Organized and clear View: The data is stored as a table in MS Excel. Hence the data looks organized and clear to understand.

10.3.2 Usage of MS Excel

MS Excel is widely used for various computational and data visualization purposes, some of the MS Excel usage is defined as follows:

Data Entry: Excel continues to be a robust platform for data entry with its grid-based interface, allowing users to input and organize data efficiently.

Time Management: Excel supports time management through date and time functions, aiding in the creation of schedules, timelines, and calendars for effective time tracking and planning.

Accounting: Excel is widely used in accounting for tasks such as creating financial statements, budgeting, and performing calculations. It provides various formulas and functions for financial analysis.

Financial analysis: Excel's analytical tools assist in in-depth financial analysis, helping users make informed decisions based on comprehensive financial insights.

Charting and Graphing: Excel offers a variety of charting and graphing options, enabling users to visually represent data for better interpretation and presentation.

Financial Modeling: Excel remains a key tool for financial modeling, allowing professionals to build intricate models for forecasting, budgeting, and scenario analysis.

Programming: With the integration of Visual Basic for Applications (VBA), Excel enables users to automate tasks, create custom functions, and develop tailored solutions to meet specific business needs.

Task Management and Data Management: Excel provides a structured environment for task and data management, allowing users to create to-do lists, track progress, and manage databases efficiently.

Customer Relationship Management (CRM): While Excel is not a dedicated CRM system, it can be adapted for basic CRM needs. Users can maintain customer databases, track interactions, and generate reports.

Mathematical Calculations: Excel is a powerful tool for mathematical computations, offering a range of built-in functions and formulas for various mathematical tasks.

Human Resource Management: Excel supports HR functions, including employee data management, payroll calculations, and performance tracking. Customizable templates and formulas simplify HR processes and reporting.

10.4 MS Power Point

Microsoft PowerPoint, usually just called the PowerPoint, is a software program developed by Microsoft to produce effective presentations. It is a part of Microsoft Office suite. The program comprises slides and various tools like word processing, drawing, graphing and outlining. Thus it can display text, table, chart, graphics and media in the slides.

10.4.1 Features of PowerPoint

Microsoft PowerPoint is a professional presentation program that allows the user to create a "presentation slide" that can be displayed on the computer screen through a projector that is plugged into the computer. There are three main features of the Microsoft PowerPoint window that you need to focus upon while learning PowerPoint. These features are Microsoft Office Button, Quick Access Toolbar and Ribbon. Some of the other important features of PowerPoint are:

Ribbon: PowerPoint has a new, intuitive user interface called the Ribbon that helps you create better presentations much more quickly than you could in earlier versions of PowerPoint.

Live Preview: PowerPoint takes advantage of the live preview feature to review your formatting choices before you apply them.

Create Dynamic Presentations: PowerPoint quickly creates dynamic and great looking presentations using the redesigned user interface and new graphics capabilities.

Video Capabilities: One of the attractive features of Microsoft PowerPoint is that it allows you to use video in your presentations. With this software, you can embed a video clip into one of your slides and use it during the slideshow. When you embed the video, you can also perform a number of editing functions which will allow you to alter the video to your needs for the presentation.

Apply a consistent look and feel in one click: PowerPoint themes help you change the look and feel of your entire presentation with just one click. PowerPoint comes with new themes, layouts and Quick Styles that offer you a wide range of options when you are formatting your presentations. Changing the theme of your presentation not only changes the background color but the color of a diagram, table etc and even the style of any bullet points within a presentation.

Sharing: Another feature of Microsoft PowerPoint is the ability to share presentations with other individuals in different locations.

Dynamically modify shapes, text, and graphics with new tools and effects: You can now manipulate and work with your text, tables, charts and other presentation elements in much richer ways than ever before.

Special Effects: When creating a presentation, one of your jobs as a presenter is to keep the attention of your audience. If you create a plain presentation without any flair, your subjects may not pay attention for long. With Microsoft PowerPoint, you can use a number of special effects to enhance the quality of your presentations.

Reduce your document sizes and improve file recovery at the same time: The new compressed Microsoft PowerPoint XML Format offers a dramatic reduction in file size, while offering an improvement in data recovery for damaged files.

Support other file formats: PowerPoint enables support for other file formats, such as PDF and XPS.

Animations and Transitions: You can add animations to elements on your slides and use transitions between slides to create smooth and visually appealing presentations.

Slide Master: PowerPoint provides a Slide Master feature that allows you to create consistent formatting and branding throughout your presentation.

Collaboration: You can collaborate on presentations with others in real-time, making it a useful tool for teamwork.

Presenter View: When presenting, PowerPoint offers a Presenter View that displays speaker notes and other useful tools on your screen while the audience sees only the presentation.

Export Options: You can save your presentations in various formats, including PowerPoint files, PDFs, and more, making it easy to share with others.

Cross-Platform Compatibility: Microsoft PowerPoint is available for both Windows and Mac platforms, ensuring broad compatibility.

10.4.2 The Importance of Effective Presentations

Effective presentations play a crucial role in various aspects of our personal and professional lives. Here's a brief description of why effective presentations are important:

Clear Communication: Presentations are a means to communicate ideas, information, and messages to an audience. A well-structured presentation ensures that your message is clear, concise, and easily understood.

Engagement: Effective presentations captivate the audience's attention. They use visual aids, storytelling, and interactive elements to engage the audience, making the content more memorable.

Impactful Storytelling: Presentations are an opportunity to tell a story that resonates with the audience. Effective storytelling can evoke emotions and drive home the main points.

Knowledge Transfer: In educational and professional settings, presentations are a common method for transferring knowledge and skills. Well-organized presentations facilitate learning and information retention.

Decision-Making: In business, presentations often play a role in decision-making processes. They provide data, analysis, and recommendations that guide choices and strategies.

Professionalism: The ability to deliver a well-prepared presentation is a sign of professionalism. It reflects competence, confidence, and preparedness, which are highly regarded in the workplace.

Influence: Effective presentations have the power to influence opinions, attitudes, and behaviors. They can persuade stakeholders, customers, and colleagues to support your ideas.

Personal Development: Developing presentation skills is a valuable personal development tool. It boosts self-confidence, public speaking skills, and the ability to convey thoughts convincingly.

Visual Appeal: Visual elements in presentations make complex information more understandable. Visuals like charts, graphs, and images enhance the overall appeal of the content.

Efficient Communication: Well-organized presentations save time and convey information efficiently. They help streamline discussions and prevent miscommunications.

10.5 MS Outlook

Microsoft Outlook is a popular and widely used email management and personal information management software developed by Microsoft. It is part of the Microsoft Office suite, which includes a range of productivity applications such as Word, Excel, and PowerPoint. Outlook is primarily known for its email functionality, but it offers a comprehensive set of tools for managing and organizing personal and professional information.

At its core, Microsoft Outlook is an email client that allows users to send, receive, and manage emails. It provides a user-friendly interface for composing, reading, and organizing emails. However, Outlook's capabilities go well beyond email.

10.5.1 Features of Microsoft Outlook

Email Management: Outlook enables users to manage multiple email accounts in one place. You can send and receive emails, set up folders to organize your messages, and use categories and flags for prioritization.

Calendar: The calendar feature in Outlook allows you to schedule and manage appointments, meetings, and events. It also supports features like reminders, recurring events, and shared calendars.

Contacts: Outlook provides a robust contact management system, allowing you to store and organize your contacts, create contact groups, and link contacts to emails and appointments.

Tasks: You can create and manage to-do lists, set task priorities, and assign tasks to others. Outlook's task management feature helps you stay organized and productive.

Notes and Journals: Users can create notes for quick reference and maintain a journal to track activities and interactions.

Customization: Outlook offers customization options for its interface, including themes, backgrounds, and email signatures. You can personalize how you interact with the software.

Integration: Outlook integrates seamlessly with other Microsoft Office applications, such as Word and Excel. It also provides integration with SharePoint and OneDrive for document and file management.

Advanced Features: Outlook includes features like conversation view, data file management (PST and OST), RSS feed support, and support for add-ins to enhance its functionality.

Outlook for Mobile and Web: In addition to the desktop version, Microsoft offers Outlook for mobile devices and a web-based version known as Outlook Web App (OWA). This allows users to access their emails and information from various platforms.

Security and Privacy: Outlook places a strong emphasis on email security and offers features like encryption, anti-phishing protection, and spam filtering.

10.5.2 Importance of Email and Communication Tools

Email and communication tools have become an integral part of both personal and professional life, and their significance cannot be overstated. These tools have revolutionized the way we interact, share information, and conduct business. Here are some key points highlighting the importance of email and communication tools:

Efficient Communication: Email provides a swift and efficient means of communication. It allows individuals and organizations to send messages and documents instantly to recipients located anywhere in the world. This speed enhances productivity and responsiveness.

Cost-Effective: Compared to traditional mail services, email is incredibly cost-effective. There are no postage fees, and communication can occur 24/7 without any additional cost.

Global Reach: Communication tools like email have eliminated geographical barriers. You can connect with people around the globe without the constraints of distance and time zones.

Document Sharing: These tools enable the easy sharing of documents, images, and other files as attachments. This feature is invaluable for collaborative work and sharing important information.

Record Keeping: Emails serve as a documented record of conversations and exchanges. This record-keeping aspect is crucial for legal and reference purposes.

Scheduling and Planning: Many communication tools, such as Microsoft Outlook, offer calendar and scheduling features. This allows users to plan meetings, set reminders, and manage their time efficiently.

Organization: Communication tools provide features like folders, labels, and categories that aid in organizing messages. This organization is especially useful when dealing with large volumes of email.

Accessibility: Emails and communication tools are accessible from various devices, including computers, smartphones, and tablets. This accessibility ensures that you can stay connected wherever you are.

Privacy and Security: Email services often incorporate encryption and security features to protect sensitive information. These tools are equipped with anti-phishing and spam filters to enhance privacy.

Business Communication: In the corporate world, email and communication tools are essential for internal and external communication. They support project collaboration, client communication, and the dissemination of official information.

Marketing and Promotion: Email marketing is a powerful tool for businesses. It allows them to reach out to a wide customer base with promotional content and updates.

Time Management: Calendar and scheduling features in communication tools help users manage their time effectively, reducing the chances of missing appointments and deadlines.\

10.6 MS Access

MS-Access is application software for managing the databases. It is released by **Microsoft** in November 1992. It actually stores the data on the basis of the **relational Jet Database Engine**. It mainly provides the graphical user interface for accessing the data and the tools for software development.

It helps the users for managing the related data more efficiently than Microsoft Excel or other applications of spreadsheets. Users can easily analyze the large amount of data stored in it.

It is not used to create large or enterprise-level databases but mainly used to create small databases. For the large databases, Microsoft provides the SQL server database engine.

10.6.1 Features of MS Access

Following are the different features or characteristics of Microsoft Access:

Any user can easily create the framework (i.e. tables) which stores the data or information in the database.

There is a **Tell Me Function** in MS Access, which allows you to create queries, tables, reports, and forms easily.

Any user can easily **import** the information in the created table of MS Access from the other applications of Microsoft.

The users who work with MS Access can easily create a **report** from the table which is selected by them. For creating a report, users need to click on the **Report Wizard** icon available in the toolbar.

One of the important features of **MS Access** is **Forms**.

Another important feature of MS Access is the **template**. Any user can use the templates which are available in software MS access.

Queries can also be considered as an essential feature of MS Access. It helps for processing the data in the tables, and for displaying the data to the users.

Microsoft Access 2010 introduced the new feature which allows the users to publish the web databases to SharePoint sites, after developing them.

A powerful feature also exists in this application software. This feature helps the developers by creating custom solutions for their databases using the **VBA (Visual Basic Application)** Code.

The users who work with Microsoft Access can easily view their reports in following different ways:

Print preview

Design View

Layout View

Report View

It also introduced the multi-valued fields. This feature allows you to select and store more than one values in one field.

10.6.2 Importance of Microsoft Access:

Those users who have a basic knowledge of computers can easily create and manage the database in Access.

It is a software program which can be used in schools for making the schedules.

Any user can easily insert the data in the database of MS Access.

It is also used to create user-friendly front ends.

In MS-Access, repetitive tasks can be easily performed by the help of macros.

Any user can access the data or information quickly with the help of commands.

It allows users for developing web applications. Various software developers also use this software for developing the application software.

This software works with the SQL Server, DB2, and Oracle databases. Because these three databases support the (ODBC) standard.

Any user can easily import data from and export data to word processing files, or spreadsheet files.

It is also used to link directly to those data which is stored in following different databases and applications:

Microsoft Excel

Text

Hypertext Mark-up Language (HTML)

Outlook

dBase

Extensible Mark-up Language (XML)

Paradox

Oracle

Microsoft SQL Server

Postgre SQL

MySQL.

10.7 MS Teams

In today's rapidly evolving work environment, the traditional office space has given way to a dynamic, technology-driven landscape where collaboration is at the forefront of productivity. The advent of digital transformation has reshaped how teams communicate, share information, and work together, and Microsoft Teams stands as a prime example of this shift. This section delves into the essential aspects of the modern workplace and how Microsoft Teams plays a pivotal role in enhancing collaboration.

10.7.1 Features of Microsoft Teams

Microsoft Teams is a versatile collaboration platform that has become indispensable in this modern work landscape. Here's how it addresses the changing needs of today's workplaces:

1. Centralized Communication: Teams combines chat, video conferencing, file sharing, and collaboration tools into one centralized platform. It acts as a single hub for all communication needs.
2. Team and Channel Structure: Teams allow users to create teams, each with its own channels, providing a structured environment for organizing discussions and content.
3. Integration with Microsoft 365: Teams seamlessly integrates with Microsoft 365, offering access to applications like Word, Excel, and SharePoint. This integration streamlines workflows and allows for real-time co-authoring of documents.
4. Mobile and Remote Access: Teams supports mobile access, making it convenient for on-the-go or remote work. Team members can collaborate and stay connected from various devices.
5. Security and Compliance: Teams prioritizes security and compliance, ensuring that sensitive information remains protected and that organizations meet regulatory requirements.
6. Third-Party App Integration: Teams supports a wide range of third-party app integrations, extending its functionality and customization possibilities.

10.7.2 Importance of Microsoft Teams

Microsoft Teams plays a pivotal role in modern workplaces, serving as a comprehensive collaboration and communication platform that goes beyond mere chat and video conferencing. In this section, we will explore in detail the multifaceted role that Microsoft Teams fulfills in enhancing productivity, streamlining communication, and fostering collaboration within organizations.

Central Hub for Communication and Collaboration

One of the fundamental roles of Microsoft Teams is to act as a centralized hub for all communication and collaboration activities. Here's how it fulfills this role:

Chat and Messaging: Teams provides a feature-rich chat and messaging environment, allowing users to engage in one-on-one chats, group chats, and team discussions. It offers real-time text-based communication, as well as the ability to share files, images, and videos within chat conversations.
Video Conferencing: Teams offers video meetings and conferencing capabilities. Users can initiate video calls, join meetings, and collaborate face-to-face with colleagues, clients, and partners regardless of their physical location. This role has become increasingly crucial in the context of remote and distributed workforces.
Team and Channel Structure: Microsoft Teams introduces a structured approach to collaboration through teams and channels. Teams serve as overarching groups for projects, departments, or cross-functional teams, while channels allow for focused discussions and content sharing within these teams.

Integration with Microsoft 365

Another vital role of Microsoft Teams is its deep integration with the Microsoft 365 ecosystem. This integration enhances productivity and streamlines workflows in several ways:

Access to Office Apps: Teams users can access and collaborate on documents, spreadsheets, and presentations using familiar Microsoft Office applications like Word, Excel, and PowerPoint. This eliminates the need to switch between different tools and applications.

OneDrive and SharePoint Integration: Files shared within Teams are seamlessly integrated with OneDrive for Business and SharePoint. This integration ensures that documents are stored securely, are accessible from anywhere, and can be collaboratively edited in real-time.

Co-Authoring Documents: Users can collaborate on documents within Teams in real-time, which is a significant advantage for projects that require simultaneous editing and reviewing of documents. Multiple team members can work on a document together, eliminating version control issues.

Enhanced Mobile and Remote Access

Microsoft Teams recognizes the importance of providing access from various devices and locations. Its role in ensuring mobile and remote access is noteworthy:

Mobile Apps: Teams offers mobile apps for iOS and Android devices, enabling team members to stay connected and collaborate on the go. Whether you're traveling or working remotely, you can participate in discussions, access files, and conduct video meetings from your smartphone or tablet.

Web Browser Access: In addition to desktop and mobile apps, Teams can be accessed via web browsers. This browser-based access allows users to participate in meetings and chats, even if they don't have the Teams app installed.

Security and Compliance

Microsoft Teams places a significant emphasis on security and compliance, making it an essential platform for organizations that handle sensitive data or operate in regulated industries. Its roles in security and compliance include:

Data Encryption: Teams ensures that data at rest and in transit is encrypted, safeguarding sensitive information from unauthorized access.

Compliance Features: It offers various compliance features and capabilities, such as eDiscovery, legal hold, and audit logs, to help organizations meet regulatory requirements.

Data Retention and Governance: Teams allows organizations to set retention policies and apply governance to their data, ensuring that information is managed in a compliant manner.

Third-Party App Integration

Microsoft Teams extends its role as a collaboration platform by supporting third-party app integrations. This role opens up a world of possibilities for customizing and extending the functionality of Teams:

App Integration: Teams can integrate with numerous third-party apps, enhancing its capabilities for project management, document sharing, and specialized workflows. Users can bring in apps like Trello, Asana, or Salesforce to streamline their work.

Bots and Automation: Users can interact with bots to automate tasks and receive information within the Teams environment, increasing efficiency and productivity.

Custom Tabs and Development: Teams allows developers to create custom tabs and extensions tailored to the specific needs of an organization. This role facilitates the creation of dedicated workspaces and tools within Teams.

Summary

A suite of productivity tools including Word, Excel, PowerPoint, and Outlook, designed for document creation, data management, communication, and presentation.

MS Word is a word processor known for text formatting, document editing, and collaboration features.

MS Excel is a spreadsheet application used for data entry, mathematical calculations, financial analysis, and data visualization.

MS PowerPoint is a presentation software for creating slideshows with text, images, charts, and multimedia.

MS Outlook is an email client with features for managing emails, calendars, contacts, and tasks.

MS Access is database management tool used for creating and managing small databases.

MS Teams is a collaboration platform combining chat, video conferencing, file sharing, and integration with Microsoft 365.

Glossary

Word Processor : Software used for creating and editing text documents (e.g., Microsoft Word).

Spreadsheet : Software used for data organization, calculation, and analysis (e.g., Microsoft Excel).

Presentation Software: Software used for creating and displaying slide presentations (e.g., Microsoft PowerPoint).

Email Client : Software used for sending, receiving, and managing emails (e.g., Microsoft Outlook).

Collaboration Platform: Software that facilitates team communication and project management (e.g., Microsoft Teams).
Pivot Table: A data summarization tool in Excel used for sorting, counting, and analyzing data.
VBA (Visual Basic for Applications): A programming language used for writing macros and automating tasks in Microsoft Office applications.

Previous Year Solved Question Paper

1. What is MS Acess Used for?[BCA 2023]
ANS: Microsoft Access is a database management system (DBMS) from Microsoft that combines the relational Microsoft Jet Database Engine with a graphical user interface and software-development tools. It is a part of the Microsoft Office suite of applications and is used for a variety of purposes:
Key Uses of Microsoft Access

Database Creation and Management:
Table Creation: Define tables to store data in a structured format.
Data Entry: Create forms for data entry, which can simplify the process and reduce data entry errors.

Data Analysis and Reporting:
Queries: Use queries to retrieve and manipulate data. Access supports SQL (Structured Query Language) for advanced data retrieval.
Reports: Design and generate reports to summarize and present data in a readable format.

Custom Application Development:
Forms and Reports: Develop custom forms and reports tailored to specific business needs.
Macros: Automate repetitive tasks using macros, which are sequences of instructions that perform specific tasks.
VBA (Visual Basic for Applications): Use VBA to write more complex and customized automation scripts and applications within Access.

Data Import and Export:
Integration with Other Applications: Import data from and export data to various formats, such as Excel, CSV, XML, and more.
Data Sharing: Share data with other databases and applications.

User Interface Design:
Navigation Forms: Create user-friendly navigation forms to facilitate user interaction with the database.
Custom Controls: Utilize a wide range of built-in controls to enhance the functionality and appearance of forms and reports.

Multi-User Support:
Database Splitting: Split the database into a front-end (user interface) and back-end (data storage) to allow multiple users to work on the database simultaneously without conflicts.
Permissions and Security: Manage user permissions to ensure data security and integrity.
Common Applications
Small to Medium-Sized Business Solutions: Ideal for small businesses that need a cost-effective way to manage data without investing in more complex DBMS systems.
Prototyping and Development: Useful for developing prototypes and proof-of-concept applications before scaling up to larger systems.
Education and Training: Used in academic settings for teaching database concepts and practical database management skills.
Personal Projects: Suitable for personal projects where users need to manage data efficiently.

2. Explain few useful function in Excel ?[BCA 2023]

ANS: Microsoft Excel offers a wide range of functions to help users perform various calculations and data analysis tasks. Here are a few useful Excel functions:

SUM
Usage: Adds a range of cells.
Syntax: =SUM(number1, [number2], ...)
Example: =SUM(A1:A10) adds all numbers in cells A1 to A10.

AVERAGE
Usage: Calculates the average of a range of cells.
Syntax: =AVERAGE(number1, [number2], ...)
Example: =AVERAGE(B1:B10) calculates the average of numbers in cells B1 to B10.

IF

Usage: Performs a logical test and returns one value for a TRUE result and another for a FALSE result.

Syntax: =IF(logical_test, value_if_true, value_if_false)

Example: =IF(C1>50, "Pass", "Fail") returns "Pass" if the value in C1 is greater than 50, otherwise "Fail".

VLOOKUP

Usage: Searches for a value in the first column of a table and returns a value in the same row from a specified column.

Syntax: =VLOOKUP(lookup_value, table_array, col_index_num, [range_lookup])

Example: =VLOOKUP(D1, A1:B10, 2, FALSE) looks up the value in D1 within the range A1and returns the corresponding value from the second column.

COUNTIF

Usage: Counts the number of cells that meet a criterion.

Syntax: =COUNTIF(range, criteria)

Example: =COUNTIF(E1:E10, ">100") counts the number of cells in the range E1that are greater than 100.

CONCATENATE (or CONCAT)

Usage: Combines multiple text strings into one string.

Syntax: =CONCATENATE(text1, [text2], ...) or =CONCAT(text1, [text2], ...)

Example: =CONCATENATE("Hello ", "World") or =CONCAT("Hello ", "World") results in "Hello World".

TEXT

Usage: Formats a number and converts it to text.

Syntax: =TEXT(value, format_text)

Example: =TEXT(1234.56, "$#,##0.00") formats the number 1234.56 as currency.

INDEX

Usage: Returns the value of an element in a table or array, selected by the row and column number indexes.

Syntax: =INDEX(array, row_num, [column_num])

Example: =INDEX(A1:C10, 2, 3) returns the value in the second row and third column of the range A1.

MATCH

Usage: Searches for a specified item in a range of cells and returns the relative position of that item.

Syntax: =MATCH(lookup_value, lookup_array, [match_type])

Example: =MATCH("Orange", A1:A10, 0) returns the position of "Orange" in the range A1.

SUMIF

Usage: Adds the cells specified by a given condition or criteria.

Syntax: =SUMIF(range, criteria, [sum_range])

Example: =SUMIF(F1:F10, ">50", G1:G10) adds the values in G1where the corresponding values in F1are greater than 50.

These functions are fundamental to leveraging Excel's powerful capabilities for data analysis, financial modeling, reporting, and more.

Previous Year Unsolved Question Paper

1. Explain few useful function in Excel ?[BCA 2023]
2. What is powerpoint presentation ?Name the features and advantages.[BCA 2023]

Exercise

Exercise 1 – Multiple Choice Questions

1. What is the primary function of Microsoft Word?
   A) Creating spreadsheets
   B) Editing images
   C) Creating and editing documents
   D) Managing emails

2. Which Microsoft Office application is used for data analysis and visualization?
   A) Word
   B) Excel
   C) PowerPoint
   D) Outlook

3. What feature in PowerPoint helps you apply a consistent look and feel to your presentation?
   A) Templates
   B) Themes
   C) Animations
   D) Transitions

4. What is the primary use of Microsoft Outlook?
   A) Creating presentations
   B) Managing emails and schedules
   C) Analyzing data
   D) Creating databases

5. Which Microsoft application is used for managing small databases?
   A) Word
   B) Excel
   C) Access
   D) PowerPoint

Exercise 2 – True/False

1. Microsoft Excel is used for creating presentations.
2. PowerPoint includes features for adding animations and transitions.
3. Outlook is part of the Microsoft Office suite and primarily handles emails.
4. The Ribbon interface is used in Microsoft Office to manage network connections.
5. Word documents can be saved as .docx files.

Exercise 3 – Fill in the blanks

1. Microsoft Word is primarily used for ______ documents.
2. Excel uses ______ to perform calculations on data.
3. PowerPoint is a software program used to create ______.
4. Outlook is known for its ______ management capabilities.
5. MS Access is used for managing ______ databases.

Exercise 4- Give Two Examples of the Following

1. Microsoft Office applications used for document creation and editing. ______________ , ______________
2. Two examples of spreadsheet functions in Excel. ______________ , ______________
3. Two features of PowerPoint for enhancing presentations. ______________ , ______________

Exercise 5- Small Answers

1. What is the primary purpose of Microsoft Word?
2. How does the AutoFill feature in Excel benefit users?
3. What is the function of the Ribbon interface in Microsoft Office?
4. Explain the importance of templates in Microsoft Word.
5. What is a Pivot Table in Excel used for?

Exercise 6- Long Answers

1. Discuss the evolution of Microsoft Word and its significance in modern document creation and editing. Include key features and their benefits to users.
2. Explain the advantages and disadvantages of using Microsoft Access for database management.

Answer

Exercise 1- 1) C , 2) B , 3) B , 4) B , 5) C
Exercise 2- 1) False , 2) True , 3) True , 4) False , 5) True
Exercise 3- 1) creating , 2)formula , 3) presentations , 4) email , 5) small

Exercise 4- 1) Microsoft Word, Microsoft OneNote,

2) SUM, VLOOKUP ,
3) Animations, Transitions ,

Exercise 5- 1)The primary purpose of Microsoft Word is to create and edit text documents such as letters, reports, and essays.

2)The AutoFill feature in Excel helps users quickly fill cells with data by recognizing patterns and extending them, saving time and reducing manual entry.

3)The Ribbon interface organizes commands into tabs and groups, making it easier for users to find and use various features in Microsoft Office applications.

4)Templates in Microsoft Word provide pre-designed document layouts, saving time and effort in formatting and ensuring a consistent and professional look.

5)A Pivot Table in Excel is used to summarize, analyze, and present data in a structured and easily understandable format, allowing users to gain insights from large datasets.

Chapter-10
TEST PAPER
Introduction to Computers

Time Duration: 30 Minutes **Maximum Marks: 25**

General Instructions:

1. The question paper consists of questions and is divided into three sections, A, B and C.
2. All questions are compulsory.
3. Section A comprises Fill in the blanks and True/False of one mark each.
4. Section B comprises question numbers 1 to 5. These are Short Question carrying two marks each.
5. Section D comprises question numbers 1. These are Long Question carrying five marks each.

SECTION-A

Fill in the blanks- **(1 X 5 = 5 marks)**

1. Microsoft ______ is a word processor used for creating and editing documents.
2. In Excel, the ______ function is used to sum up a range of cells.
3. Microsoft ______ is used for creating slide presentations.
4. The ______ view in PowerPoint helps presenters by displaying notes and tools while presenting.
5. Microsoft ______ is a database management system used for creating and managing small databases.

True/False- **(1 X 5 = 5 marks)**

1. Microsoft Excel can be used for financial analysis and data visualization.
2. MS Outlook is primarily used for creating presentations.
3. OneDrive is Microsoft's cloud storage service.
4. Macros in MS Excel are used to automate repetitive tasks.
5. MS Word does not support real-time collaboration.

SECTION-B

Short Question- **(2 X 5 = 10 marks)**

1. What is the primary use of Microsoft Excel?
2. How does Microsoft Word assist in document formatting?
3. What is the Ribbon interface in Microsoft Office applications?
4. Explain the importance of templates in MS Word.
5. What role does Microsoft Teams play in modern workplaces?

SECTION-C

Long Question- . **(5 marks)**

1. Discuss the evolution of Microsoft Word and its significance in document creation and editing. Explain key features and how they benefit users.

ONLINE RESOURCES

Chapter 10 Practice Paper
Link
https://forms.gle/17qbGTHStNjKDmDp8

Chapter 10 Video Content
Link
https://youtu.be/7DeMPFN3E2s?si=qQwYXbTpHQmzf-bF
QR Code

Chapter 11: Social Media

In this chapter you will learn about :

- Defining Social Media
- Historical Overview
- Types of Social Media Platforms
- The Major Social Media Platforms' role
- The Role of Social Media in Modern Communication

11.1 Defining Social Media

Social media has become an integral part of our daily lives, revolutionizing the way we connect, communicate, and share information. While its roots can be traced back to the early days of the internet, the term "social media" has evolved and expanded over the years, encompassing a wide array of platforms and functions. In this comprehensive exploration, we will delve into the multifaceted nature of social media, its evolution, and its impact on society. At its core, social media refers to digital platforms and applications that enable individuals and groups to create, share, and interact with content. This content can take various forms, including text, images, videos, and links, and it is typically shared within a user's network or made publicly accessible. Key features of social media include user-generated content, real-time interactions, and the ability to form connections with others based on common interests or affiliations.

The roots of social media can be traced back to the early days of online communities and forums, where individuals gathered to discuss shared interests and exchange information. However, the concept of social media as we know it today began to take shape with the emergence of platforms like Friendster and My Space in the early 2000s. These platforms allowed users to create profiles, connect with friends, and share personal updates and media.

The real turning point in the evolution of social media came with the launch of Facebook in 2004. Mark Zuckerberg's creation revolutionized the way we interacted online by introducing features such as the News Feed, which displayed a curated stream of content from users' friends and pages they followed. This innovation marked the transition from static profiles to dynamic, content-driven platforms.

Today, social media encompasses a vast and diverse ecosystem of platforms, including but not limited to Facebook, Twitter, Instagram, LinkedIn, Tik-Tok, Snapchat, and YouTube. Each platform caters to specific user demographics and preferences, offering unique features and functionalities. For instance, Instagram focuses on visual storytelling through photos and short videos, while LinkedIn is geared towards professional networking and career development.

The impact of social media on society is profound and multifaceted. On one hand, it has democratized information dissemination, enabling individuals and organizations to reach a global audience with their messages. It has also facilitated the formation of online communities, allowing like-minded individuals to connect, share knowledge, and provide support.

However, social media is not without its challenges and controversies. Issues such as privacy concerns, cyberbullying, and the spread of misinformation have garnered significant attention. The addictive nature of these platforms and their potential to negatively impact mental health are also subjects of ongoing debate and research.

In conclusion, social media is a complex and ever-evolving phenomenon that has redefined how we communicate and connect in the digital age. It encompasses a wide range of platforms, each with its own unique characteristics, and has both positive and negative impacts on society. As social media continues to evolve, it is essential for individuals, organizations, and policymakers to navigate its intricacies and harness its potential while addressing its challenges responsibly.

Top of Form

11.2 Historical Overview

The history of social media is a journey through the digital landscape, marked by significant milestones that have transformed the way we communicate, share information, and connect with others. From the humble beginnings of online forums to the global phenomenon of today's social media giants, this historical overview delves into the evolution of social media, highlighting key developments and their impact on society.

The concept of social media has its roots in the early days of the internet, when people started connecting through online communities and bulletin board systems (BBS) in the 1970s and 1980s. These early platforms allowed individuals to exchange messages and share information with others who shared similar interests, laying the groundwork for the social interaction that would follow. The 1990s witnessed the emergence of platforms like Six Degrees and Friendster. Six Degrees, launched in 1997, is often considered the first recognizable social media platform. It allowed users to create profiles and list their friends, thus forming a rudimentary social network. Friendster, introduced in 2002, followed a similar model, but its popularity was limited due to technical issues.

The turning point in the history of social media came in the mid-2000s with the launch of platforms that would go on to shape the industry. In 2004, Mark Zuckerberg and his colleagues launched Facebook from a Harvard dorm room. Initially exclusive to college students, Facebook quickly gained traction and expanded to a wider user base, introducing features such as the News Feed and the ability to share multimedia content.

2006 marked the birth of Twitter, a microblogging platform that allowed users to share short text updates (tweets) with their followers. Twitter's real-time nature and simplicity made it a powerful tool for breaking news and fostering global conversations. The late 2000s saw the rise of visual platforms like Instagram and Pinterest. Instagram, founded in 2010, revolutionized photo sharing with its user-friendly interface and filters, while Pinterest became a hub for visual inspiration and idea-sharing. The video-sharing platform YouTube, launched in 2005, became a cultural phenomenon, allowing individuals and creators to share videos with a global audience. It gave rise to a new generation of online celebrities and content creators. In 2010, the Chinese platform WeChat combined social networking with messaging services, becoming a comprehensive communication tool. Meanwhile, Snapchat introduced ephemeral messaging, appealing to younger users who sought more private and playful interactions.

The 2010s also witnessed the explosive growth of Tik-Tok, a short-form video platform that gained massive popularity for its viral challenges and user-generated content. It became a hub for creativity and self-expression among young audiences.

The historical overview of social media would be incomplete without mentioning the professional networking platform LinkedIn, which launched in 2003. LinkedIn provided a platform for job seekers, professionals, and businesses to connect, network, and collaborate.

As social media continued to evolve, it brought about significant societal changes. It transformed the way businesses market their products, influenced political discourse, and provided a platform for social activism and movements. However, it also raised concerns about privacy, data security, and the spread of misinformation.

In conclusion, the history of social media is a testament to the power of digital innovation in reshaping human communication and connectivity. From the early days of online forums to the global reach of today's social media giants, this journey reflects our ever-evolving relationship with technology and our insatiable desire to connect with others in the digital age. As social media continues to evolve, its impact on society will undoubtedly continue to evolve as well, posing both challenges and opportunities for individuals and communities worldwide.

Top of Form

11.3 Types of Social Media Platforms

The landscape of social media platforms is vast and diverse, catering to various communication styles, interests, and demographics. From the inception of the internet to the present day, a multitude of social media platforms have emerged, each offering unique features and functionalities. This comprehensive overview will explore the different types of social media platforms, categorizing them based on their primary purposes and use cases.

11.3.1 Social Networking Platforms:

Facebook: Founded in 2004, Facebook is the quintessential social networking platform, connecting friends and family, and allowing users to share updates, photos, and videos. It has evolved into a multifunctional platform with groups, pages, and marketplace features.

LinkedIn: Launched in 2003, LinkedIn is a professional networking platform designed for job seekers, professionals, and businesses. It facilitates career networking, job postings, and industry-related discussions.

11.3.2 Microblogging Platforms:

Twitter: Introduced in 2006, Twitter enables users to post short, 280-character messages called tweets. It has become a hub for real-time news updates, discussions, and hashtag-driven conversations.

11.3.3 Visual Content Sharing Platforms:

Instagram: Founded in 2010, Instagram focuses on visual content sharing, allowing users to post and explore photos and short videos. Features like Stories and IGTV enhance its appeal to creators and influencers.

Pinterest: Launched in 2010, Pinterest serves as a virtual pin board for discovering and sharing images, ideas, and inspiration, making it a valuable resource for DIY enthusiasts, decorators, and fashionistas.

11.3.4 Video Sharing Platforms:

YouTube: Established in 2005, YouTube is the largest video-sharing platform globally. It hosts a wide range of video content, from educational tutorials to entertainment and vlogs.

TikTok: Emerging in 2016, TikTok is known for its short-form video content, often featuring music and creative challenges. It has quickly gained popularity among younger audiences.

11.3.5 Messaging and Chat Platforms:

WhatsApp: Acquired by Facebook in 2014, WhatsApp is a widely-used messaging app that enables text, voice, and video communication among users, both one-on-one and in groups.

Messenger: Facebook's Messenger app offers instant messaging, voice calls, and video chats within the Facebook ecosystem.

11.3.6 Professional and Business Platforms:

Slack: Launched in 2013, Slack is a messaging platform designed for teams and workplaces, facilitating collaboration, file sharing, and project management.

GitHub: GitHub, established in 2008, is a platform for software developers to collaborate on code, manage repositories, and track changes.

11.3.7 Location-Based Platforms:

Foursquare: Introduced in 2009, Foursquare is a location-based social platform that enables users to check in at places, leave reviews, and discover local businesses and attractions.

11.3.8 Niche and Specialized Platforms:

Reddit: Founded in 2005, Reddit is a community-driven platform organized into thousands of topic-based subreddits. It encourages discussions and content sharing on virtually any subject.

Goodreads: Goodreads, established in 2007, focuses on books and reading, allowing users to share book recommendations, reviews, and reading lists.

11.3.9 Audio and Podcasting Platforms:

Sound Cloud: Founded in 2007, Sound Cloud is a platform for sharing and discovering music, audio recordings, and podcasts.

Clubhouse: Launched in 2020, Clubhouse is an audio-based social network that facilitates live discussions and conversations.

11.4 The Major Social Media Platforms' role in daily life

Social media has become an integral part of our daily lives, profoundly impacting the way we communicate, connect, and consume information. Platforms like Facebook, Twitter, Instagram, LinkedIn, and many others have transformed the way we interact with the world around us. Below, we delve into the multifaceted roles that social media plays in our daily routines.

11.4.1 Communication and Connection

Communication and connection are fundamental aspects of human existence. They form the bedrock of our relationships, societies, and the very fabric of our daily lives. In this era of advanced technology and digital interconnectedness, the dynamics of communication and connection have evolved significantly, both in terms of their reach and complexity.

The Evolution of Communication: Throughout history, humans have continuously sought ways to communicate over distances, transcending geographical barriers. From the earliest cave paintings to the invention of the printing press, our need to share ideas, emotions, and information has driven innovation. The digital age has ushered in a new era of communication, with a wide array of tools and platforms at our disposal.

Social Media and Online Communication: One of the most transformative developments in contemporary communication is the rise of social media. Platforms like Facebook, Twitter, Instagram, and LinkedIn have fundamentally altered how we interact and connect with others. These platforms facilitate instant communication with friends, family, and acquaintances, regardless of geographical locations. They enable us to share our experiences, thoughts, and emotions in real-time, fostering a sense of closeness even when miles apart.

Global Connectivity: The internet has made the world a global village, bringing together people from diverse cultures and backgrounds. This global connectivity has broadened our horizons, exposing us to a wealth of perspectives and ideas. It has also enabled collaboration and cooperation on a global scale, from international business ventures to humanitarian efforts.

Challenges in Digital Communication: While digital communication has enriched our lives in numerous ways, it has also presented challenges. The absence of face-to-face interactions can sometimes lead to misunderstandings or misinterpretations. Additionally, the constant connectivity provided by smartphones and social media can create a sense of digital overload, affecting mental well-being.

The Importance of In-Person Interaction: In the midst of this digital revolution, it's crucial to remember the irreplaceable value of in-person communication. Face-to-face interactions offer a depth and richness that cannot be fully replicated in the digital realm. They allow for nuances in tone, body language, and facial expressions, enhancing the quality of our connections.

Fostering Meaningful Relationships: Meaningful connections are built on trust, empathy, and genuine human interaction. While social media and digital tools facilitate initial contact and maintain connections, they should complement, not replace, in-person interactions. In our busy lives, setting aside time for face-to-face meetings with friends, family, and colleagues can help nurture and deepen these essential relationships.

Professional Connections and Networking: In the professional sphere, personal connections and networking remain pivotal. While platforms like LinkedIn provide digital spaces for networking, in-person meetings at conferences, seminars, and industry events continue to be invaluable. Building professional relationships through genuine interactions often leads to career opportunities and collaborations that transcend the virtual realm.

11Top of Form

11.4.2 Information and News

In the digital age, the dissemination and consumption of information and news have undergone a profound transformation. The internet, social media, and digital platforms have fundamentally changed the way we access, share, and interact with news and information. While these changes have brought about many benefits, they have also presented new challenges and considerations.

The Digital Information Landscape: The digital era has democratized access to information and news like never before. With a few clicks, individuals can access a vast array of information sources, from traditional news outlets to independent bloggers and citizen journalists. This democratization has empowered individuals to be more informed and engaged in current events, fostering a more active and informed citizenry.

Real-Time News and Updates: One of the most significant advantages of the digital age is the ability to receive real-time news and updates. Social media platforms like Twitter have become real-time newsfeeds, allowing users to stay updated on breaking news stories as they unfold. This immediate access to information enhances our ability to respond to events, whether they are global news or local emergencies.

Diverse Perspectives and Opinions: Digital platforms have made it easier for diverse perspectives and opinions to be heard. People can follow news sources and commentators who align with their viewpoints or seek out alternative voices, leading to a more pluralistic media landscape. This diversity of perspectives encourages critical thinking and a deeper understanding of complex issues.

Challenges in the Digital Information Age: While the digital information age has brought about significant advantages, it has also posed several challenges:

Misinformation and Disinformation: The ease of publishing on the internet has made it possible for false or misleading information to spread rapidly. Misinformation and disinformation campaigns can have real-world consequences, including public health crises and social discord.

Information Overload: With the abundance of information available, individuals may experience information overload. It can be challenging to sift through vast amounts of data to find accurate and relevant information.

Filter Bubbles and Echo Chambers: Digital algorithms on social media platforms often show users content that aligns with their existing beliefs. This can lead to filter bubbles and echo chambers, where people are exposed primarily to information that reinforces their pre-existing views, limiting exposure to diverse perspectives.

Trust in News Sources: The proliferation of unreliable news sources and the prevalence of fake news have eroded trust in traditional media outlets. Distinguishing credible sources from unreliable ones has become a critical skill for information consumers.

Media Literacy and Critical Thinking: In the digital information age, media literacy and critical thinking skills are more important than ever. Educating individuals about how to evaluate sources, fact-check information, and discern between credible and unreliable content is essential for responsible information consumption.

The Role of Traditional Journalism: Despite the challenges, traditional journalism remains a cornerstone of reliable news and information. Established news organizations adhere to journalistic standards of accuracy, objectivity, and ethics. High-quality journalism serves as a vital counterbalance to the proliferation of misinformation and disinformation.

- Top of Form

11.4.3 Personal Expression

Personal expression is the profound act of conveying one's thoughts, feelings, beliefs, and identity to the world. It encompasses various forms of creative and communicative outlets, allowing individuals to showcase their uniqueness and connect with others on a deeper level. In this digital age, personal expression has taken on new dimensions, offering countless avenues for individuals to share their voices and perspectives.

Forms of Personal Expression: Personal expression can manifest in numerous ways, including:

Visual Arts: Painting, drawing, sculpture, and photography are traditional forms of visual personal expression. They allow individuals to convey their emotions, perspectives, and creativity through visual imagery.

Writing: Writing is a powerful medium for personal expression. It encompasses various forms such as journaling, poetry, fiction, and essays, enabling individuals to articulate their thoughts and emotions with precision and depth.

Fashion and Style: The way we dress and present ourselves is a visual representation of our personal expression. Fashion choices, hairstyles, and accessories can communicate individuality, cultural influences, and personal tastes.

Music: Music is a universal language of personal expression. Composing, performing, or even simply listening to music can convey emotions and stories, connecting people on an emotional level.

Dance and Movement: Dance is a kinetic form of personal expression. It allows individuals to convey emotions, tell stories, and communicate cultural traditions through movement.

Social Media and Digital Content: In the digital age, social media platforms, blogs, and vlogs provide a platform for personal expression on a global scale. Users can share their thoughts, experiences, and creative works with a vast online audience.

The Digital Age and Personal Expression: The advent of the internet and digital technology has significantly expanded the scope of personal expression. Online platforms have democratized the ability to share one's voice and creativity with a global audience. Social media platforms like Instagram, YouTube, and TikTok allow individuals to showcase their talents, share their stories, and connect with like-minded individuals.

Benefits of Digital Personal Expression:

Global Reach: Digital platforms provide a global stage for personal expression. Content creators can connect with people from diverse cultures and backgrounds, fostering cross-cultural understanding and collaboration.

Community Building: Online communities centered around specific interests or causes have flourished. These communities provide a sense of belonging and support for individuals who may not find such connections in their immediate physical surroundings.

Career Opportunities: Many individuals have turned their personal expression into successful careers. Content creators, influencers, and digital artists have found avenues for monetizing their creative work.

Amplification of Marginalized Voices: The digital space has given marginalized and underrepresented groups a platform to amplify their voices, share their experiences, and advocate for change.

Challenges of Digital Personal Expression:

While digital personal expression offers numerous benefits, it also comes with challenges:

Digital Overload: The constant connectivity and information saturation online can lead to digital overload and burnout.

Privacy Concerns: Sharing personal information and creative work online may raise privacy and security concerns.

Validation and Comparison: The pursuit of likes, shares, and validation can lead to unhealthy comparisons and self-esteem issues.

11.4.4 Professional Networking

Professional networking is a fundamental component of career development and success. It involves the deliberate cultivation of relationships and connections with individuals in one's industry or field of interest. These connections can open doors to opportunities, offer valuable insights, and provide support throughout one's professional journey. In today's interconnected world, the importance of professional networking cannot be overstated.

Why Professional Networking Matters:

Access to Opportunities: Networking allows individuals to tap into the hidden job market. Many job openings and career opportunities are never publicly advertised but are instead filled through referrals and recommendations. Networking increases your chances of learning about and securing these opportunities.

Knowledge Sharing: Interacting with professionals in your field provides opportunities to exchange insights, best practices, and industry trends. Learning from the experiences of others can help you stay informed and stay ahead in your career.

Mentorship and Guidance: Networking can connect you with mentors and experienced professionals who can provide guidance and advice. A mentor can offer invaluable insights and help you navigate the complexities of your chosen profession.

Building a Personal Brand: Effective networking allows you to showcase your skills, expertise, and personal brand. When you consistently engage with your professional network, you become known for your capabilities, increasing your visibility and credibility.

Collaboration and Partnerships: Networking can lead to collaboration opportunities and partnerships. Working with others in your industry can result in innovative projects, shared resources, and mutually beneficial ventures.

Strategies for Effective Professional Networking:

Set Clear Goals: Define your networking objectives. Are you looking for a mentor, job opportunities, or industry insights? Having clear goals will help you focus your efforts.

Attend Industry Events: Conferences, seminars, workshops, and networking events are excellent opportunities to meet professionals in your field. Be proactive in seeking out these events and participate actively.

Leverage Online Platforms: Social media and professional networking platforms like LinkedIn offer a convenient way to connect with industry peers. Optimize your online profile, join relevant groups, and engage in meaningful discussions.

Build Genuine Relationships: Networking is not just about collecting business cards or adding connections on LinkedIn. It's about building authentic relationships based on trust and mutual benefit. Be genuinely interested in others and their experiences.

Follow Up: After meeting someone at an event or connecting online, be sure to follow up. Send a personalized message or email expressing your interest in continuing the conversation. Consistent follow-up helps maintain relationships.

Give before You Receive: Networking is a two-way street. Offer your expertise, assistance, or resources to others in your network without expecting immediate reciprocation. Building goodwill can lead to long-term, fruitful relationships.

Overcoming Networking Challenges: Networking can be daunting for some individuals. Common challenges include:

Introversion: If you're naturally introverted, networking can feel overwhelming. Start by attending smaller events, preparing talking points, and setting realistic goals for interactions.

Time Constraints: Many professionals struggle to find time for networking amidst busy schedules. Prioritize networking by allocating specific time in your calendar for it.

Fear of Rejection: The fear of rejection can hold individuals back from initiating conversations. Remember that not every interaction will result in a profound connection, and rejection is a natural part of networking.

Top of Form

11.4.5 Entertainment and Leisure

Entertainment and leisure activities play a pivotal role in our lives, providing us with opportunities to relax, unwind, and find joy in the midst of our busy schedules. These moments of respite are essential for maintaining physical and mental well-being, fostering creativity, and enhancing the quality of life. In this article, we will explore the significance of entertainment and leisure in our daily lives and the various ways in which we can make the most of these precious moments.

The Importance of Entertainment and Leisure:

Stress Reduction: Entertainment and leisure activities offer a much-needed break from the stresses and demands of daily life. Whether it's watching a movie, reading a book, or enjoying a hobby, these activities help reduce stress and promote relaxation.

Mental Health: Engaging in enjoyable leisure pursuits is closely linked to improved mental health. It can alleviate symptoms of anxiety and depression, boost mood, and enhance overall well-being.

Creativity and Inspiration: Leisure activities often stimulate creativity and inspire new ideas. When we engage in activities we are passionate about, our minds are free to wander, making space for innovative thoughts and solutions.

Building Relationships: Entertainment and leisure activities provide opportunities to connect with family and friends. Sharing these experiences fosters deeper bonds and creates lasting memories.

Physical Health: Some forms of leisure, such as sports and outdoor activities, contribute to physical fitness and well-being. Maintaining an active lifestyle through leisure pursuits is essential for a healthy body.

Types of Entertainment and Leisure Activities:

Reading: Whether it's novels, magazines, or non-fiction books, reading offers an immersive escape into different worlds, cultures, and ideas.

Movies and TV Shows: Watching films and television series is a popular form of entertainment. It allows us to explore diverse genres, narratives, and perspectives.

Outdoor Activities: Activities like hiking, biking, camping, and gardening provide opportunities to connect with nature, get exercise, and rejuvenate the mind.

Art and Creativity: Engaging in creative pursuits such as painting, drawing, writing, or crafting allows individuals to express themselves artistically and tap into their imagination.

Music: Playing musical instruments, attending concerts, or simply listening to music can be a source of relaxation and enjoyment.

Sports and Games: Participating in sports, board games, or video games offers opportunities for competition, strategy, and camaraderie.

Balancing Work and Leisure: In today's fast-paced world, finding the right balance between work and leisure can be challenging. However, it is crucial for overall well-being and productivity. Here are some strategies to achieve this balance:

Prioritize Leisure: Make leisure a priority in your life by scheduling regular time for it in your calendar. Treat it as an essential part of self-care.

Set Boundaries: Establish clear boundaries between work and leisure. Avoid checking work emails or taking work-related calls during your leisure time.

Variety of Activities: Explore a variety of leisure activities to keep things fresh and exciting. Trying new things can ignite passion and creativity.

Quality over Quantity: It's not about the amount of leisure time but the quality of it. Aim for meaningful and fulfilling leisure activities that truly relax and rejuvenate you.

Unplug: Disconnect from digital devices during leisure time to fully immerse yourself in the experience. Overreliance on screens can detract from the quality of leisure.

Share with Others: Engage in leisure activities with friends or family to strengthen relationships and create shared experiences.

Top of Form

11.4.6 Business and Marketing

Business and marketing are inextricably linked disciplines that are fundamental to the success and growth of any organization. In the dynamic and competitive landscape of today's global economy, businesses must effectively navigate the intricacies of marketing to reach their target audiences, drive sales, and establish a strong brand presence. In this article, we will explore the essential role of business and marketing and how they intersect to drive growth and profitability.

Business: The Foundation of Success: At its core, a business is an organization that offers products or services to meet the needs and wants of customers. It encompasses a wide range of activities, including product development, operations, finance, human resources, and more. Successful businesses operate efficiently and strategically, focusing on the following key aspects:

Value Proposition: Businesses must define and communicate their unique value proposition — what sets them apart from competitors and why customers should choose their products or services.

Customer-Centric Approach: Understanding and addressing customer needs is paramount. Businesses that prioritize customer satisfaction tend to build loyal customer bases and benefit from repeat business.

Innovation and Adaptation: In a rapidly changing world, businesses must continually innovate and adapt to evolving market conditions, technologies, and consumer preferences.

Financial Management: Sound financial management, including budgeting, forecasting, and risk management, is essential for business sustainability and growth.

Operational Efficiency: Streamlining operations, optimizing supply chains, and minimizing waste contribute to cost efficiency and profitability.

Marketing: The Art of Connection: Marketing is the strategic process of creating, promoting, and delivering value to customers, clients, and stakeholders. It involves various activities aimed at understanding consumer behavior, building brand awareness, and driving customer engagement. Effective marketing strategies can elevate a business's visibility, credibility, and revenue through the following key components:

Market Research: Thorough market research helps businesses understand their target audience, their needs, and their preferences. This information informs product development and marketing strategies.

Brand Building: Establishing a strong brand identity creates recognition, trust, and loyalty among customers. A compelling brand story and consistent messaging are essential elements.

Digital Marketing: In the digital age, online marketing channels, such as social media, content marketing, email marketing, and search engine optimization (SEO), play a pivotal role in reaching and engaging with customers.

Advertising and Promotion: Marketing campaigns, both online and offline, are designed to promote products or services, drive sales, and raise brand awareness.

Customer Relationship Management (CRM): Maintaining positive relationships with customers through personalized communication and excellent customer service is crucial for customer retention and advocacy.

The Interplay between Business and Marketing: The relationship between business and marketing is symbiotic. Effective marketing strategies align with and support business objectives, ensuring that resources are allocated wisely to achieve growth and profitability. Here's how they intersect:

Market Orientation: Businesses that adopt a market-oriented approach focus on customer needs and preferences, using marketing insights to guide product development and business decisions.

Revenue Generation: Marketing efforts are instrumental in generating sales and revenue. Marketing teams create and execute campaigns that attract leads, convert prospects into customers, and retain loyal clients.

Strategic Planning: Marketing plans are integral to a business's strategic planning process. They provide a roadmap for achieving business goals and objectives.

Feedback Loop: Marketing channels and customer interactions provide valuable feedback to businesses. This feedback informs product improvements, service enhancements, and overall business strategy.

Competitive Advantage: Businesses can gain a competitive advantage through effective marketing strategies. Marketing helps differentiate products or services in the market and positions them favorably against competitors.

Top of Form

11.4.7 Activism and Advocacy

Activism and advocacy are powerful vehicles for driving positive change in society. They are rooted in the principles of social and political engagement, with the aim of raising awareness, mobilizing support, and effecting meaningful transformation. In this article, we will explore the essential role of activism and advocacy, their impact on various societal issues, and the methods employed by activists and advocates to make a difference.

Understanding Activism and Advocacy:

Activism is the practice of taking deliberate action to bring about social, political, economic, or environmental change. Activists are individuals or groups who passionately advocate for a specific cause or issue. They often engage in activities such as protests, demonstrations, and grassroots organizing to raise awareness and drive change.

Advocacy, on the other hand, involves supporting or promoting a particular cause or issue through various means, including lobbying, education, and public awareness campaigns. Advocates work within existing systems and institutions to influence policies, legislation, and public opinion.

The Importance of Activism and Advocacy:

Giving a Voice to the Voiceless: Activists and advocates often champion the rights and interests of marginalized or underrepresented groups who may not have the resources or platforms to advocate for themselves.

Driving Social Change: Activism and advocacy have played pivotal roles in advancing civil rights, gender equality, environmental protection, and numerous other social justice issues.

Holding Institutions Accountable: Activists and advocates serve as watchdogs, holding governments, corporations, and institutions accountable for their actions and policies.

Raising Awareness: They shine a spotlight on critical issues, helping to educate the public and generate empathy and support for various causes.

Fostering Dialogue: Activism and advocacy foster constructive dialogue and debate, encouraging society to confront pressing issues and explore potential solutions.

Examples of Activism and Advocacy:

Civil Rights Movement: The U.S. Civil Rights Movement of the 1950s and 1960s was a pivotal period of activism that sought to end racial segregation and discrimination. Leaders like Martin Luther King Jr. and organizations like the NAACP used nonviolent protest and advocacy to drive change.

Environmental Advocacy: Environmental activists and advocates have been instrumental in raising awareness about climate change, biodiversity loss, and pollution. They work to influence policies, promote conservation efforts, and encourage sustainable practices.

Gender Equality: Activists and advocates in the feminist movement have fought for gender equality, reproductive rights, and an end to gender-based violence. Their efforts have led to legal reforms, greater workplace inclusion, and cultural shifts.

LGBTQ+ Rights: LGBTQ+ activists and advocates have campaigned for equal rights, marriage equality, and an end to discrimination. Their work has resulted in significant legal advancements and increased acceptance and visibility.

Methods of Activism and Advocacy:

Protests and Demonstrations: Public rallies, marches, and protests are common forms of activism. They draw attention to specific issues and can create momentum for change.

Lobbying: Advocates engage with policymakers to influence legislation and policies that align with their causes. This often involves meetings with legislators and strategic communication efforts.

Education and Awareness Campaigns: Activists and advocates use educational campaigns, media outreach, and social media to inform the public about critical issues and garner support.

Legal Action: Some activists and advocates resort to legal action to challenge policies, regulations, or practices that they believe are unjust.

Coalitions and Alliances: Many organizations form coalitions and alliances to amplify their voices and pool resources for advocacy efforts.

Challenges and Impact:

Challenges: Activists and advocates often face obstacles such as resistance from those in power, public apathy, and threats to their safety. Additionally, achieving lasting change can be a slow and challenging process.

Impact: Despite these challenges, activism and advocacy have a demonstrable impact on society. They have led to significant policy changes, cultural shifts, and improvements in the lives of countless individuals and communities.

Top of Form

11.4.8 Learning and Education

Social media has become an integral part of our daily lives, influencing how we communicate, share information, and connect with others. Beyond its role in socializing and entertainment, social media has emerged as a powerful tool for learning and education. In this article, we will explore the impact of social media on learning and education, its advantages, challenges, and the evolving landscape of digital education.

The Role of Social Media in Learning and Education: Social media platforms, such as Facebook, Twitter, Instagram, LinkedIn, and YouTube, have transcended their initial purposes and have found applications in the realm of learning and education. Here are some of the key ways social media is shaping education:

Informal Learning: Social media platforms serve as informal learning spaces, where users can access a wealth of information, news, articles, and videos on a wide range of topics. They provide a dynamic and interactive environment for self-directed learning.

Collaborative Learning: Social media enables collaborative learning experiences. Students and educators can create online communities, share resources, discuss topics, and collaborate on projects, breaking down geographical barriers.

Professional Development: Platforms like LinkedIn are instrumental for professional development and networking. Users can connect with peers, join industry-specific groups, and access a wealth of resources to enhance their skills and knowledge.

Blended Learning: Many educational institutions incorporate social media into their curriculum as a part of blended learning approaches. Social media can supplement traditional classroom instruction by providing additional resources and fostering discussions.

Global Reach: Social media connects learners and educators across the globe. It provides access to diverse perspectives, cultures, and experiences, enriching the educational journey.

Advantages of Learning through Social Media:

Accessibility: Social media platforms are accessible to a broad audience, making education and learning resources available to people of all ages and backgrounds.

Flexibility: Learning through social media is flexible, allowing learners to access content at their own pace and convenience.

Engagement: The interactive nature of social media can enhance engagement. Multimedia content, discussion forums, and real-time interactions can make learning more stimulating.

Resource Sharing: Users can easily share educational content, articles, videos, and other resources, curating personalized learning experiences.

Real-World Application: Social media can bridge the gap between theoretical knowledge and real-world application by facilitating discussions, case studies, and practical examples.

Challenges and Considerations: While social media offers numerous benefits for learning and education, it also presents challenges and considerations:

Digital Literacy: Not all users are proficient in digital literacy, which can hinder their ability to navigate and critically evaluate the vast amount of information available on social media.

Privacy and Security: Privacy concerns and issues related to data security on social media platforms can be a barrier to adoption, particularly in educational settings.

Distraction: The same features that make social media engaging can also be distracting. Maintaining focus on educational content can be a challenge.

Quality Control: The quality of educational content on social media can vary widely. It is essential to critically assess the credibility and reliability of sources.

The Future of Learning and Education through Social Media: The role of social media in education is likely to continue evolving. Some potential future developments include:

Personalized Learning: Social media algorithms could be further refined to provide personalized learning experiences tailored to individual needs and preferences.

Virtual Reality (VR) and Augmented Reality (AR): The integration of VR and AR technologies with social media platforms could create immersive educational experiences.

Data Analytics: Advanced data analytics could be used to track learner progress and adapt content to meet their specific learning needs.

Micro learning: Short, bite-sized educational content, such as videos and infographics, is likely to become even more prevalent on social media.

Top of Form

Top of Form

7.5 The Role of Social Media in Modern Communication

In the 21st century, social media has emerged as a transformative force in the realm of communication. It has revolutionized the way individuals, businesses, and societies interact, share information, and engage with one another. This essay explores the pivotal role of social media in modern communication, highlighting its impact on personal connections, businesses, politics, and society as a whole.

Social media platforms have become an integral part of daily life, enabling people to stay connected with friends and family regardless of geographical distances. It fosters a sense of community and provides a space for personal expression. Individuals can share updates, photos, and videos, allowing loved ones to stay updated on their lives. The real-time nature of platforms like Facebook, Instagram, and Twitter makes it easy to maintain ongoing conversations, making long-distance relationships more manageable.

Furthermore, social media plays a crucial role in business communication. It has transformed the way companies interact with their customers, market their products, and build brand identity. Businesses can engage with their audience directly, gathering feedback and addressing concerns promptly. Platforms like Instagram and Pinterest allow for visual storytelling, while LinkedIn facilitates professional networking and recruitment. Social media advertising has become a potent tool for reaching target demographics and measuring campaign success, making it a staple in modern marketing strategies.

In the realm of politics, social media has redefined political communication and activism. It offers politicians and political parties a direct channel to communicate with constituents and mobilize supporters. Barack Obama's successful 2008 presidential campaign, which heavily relied on social media, is a notable example. Social media platforms also serve as spaces for political discourse and social activism, giving a voice to marginalized groups and sparking important discussions on issues such as racial justice, climate change, and human rights. Movements like #BlackLivesMatter and #MeToo have gained global traction through social media.

However, the impact of social media on modern communication is not without challenges and controversies. The spread of misinformation, fake news, and echo chambers are significant concerns. Algorithms on platforms like Facebook and Twitter may inadvertently amplify extreme viewpoints, reinforcing existing biases. Additionally, privacy breaches and data misuse have raised questions about the security of personal information on these platforms.

Social media also influences the way we consume news and information. Many individuals rely on platforms like Twitter and Reddit for breaking news and updates, often bypassing traditional media outlets. While this provides rapid access to information, it also raises concerns about the accuracy and credibility of sources.

The role of social media in shaping public opinion and influencing elections has garnered significant attention. The spread of disinformation campaigns and foreign interference in elections has led to calls for increased regulation and transparency on these platforms.

In conclusion, social media has become an indispensable tool in modern communication, reshaping personal connections, business practices, politics, and societal discourse. Its ability to foster connectivity, facilitate information sharing, and mobilize communities is unparalleled. However, its impact is not without challenges, including issues related to misinformation, privacy, and the influence on public opinion. As social media continues to evolve, its role in modern communication will undoubtedly remain a subject of ongoing debate and scrutiny, as individuals, businesses, and policymakers grapple with its opportunities and challenges.

Summary

Social Media is digital platforms for content creation, sharing, and interaction.
Evolution from early online communities to modern platforms like Facebook and Twitter.
Includes social networking, microblogging, visual content sharing, video sharing, messaging, and more.
It Communication, information dissemination, personal expression, professional networking, entertainment, business marketing, activism, and education.
Modern Communication is integral for personal connections, business marketing, political communication, and social activism.

Glossary

Microblogging: Posting short updates or messages.
Visual Content Sharing: Platforms for photos and videos (e.g., Instagram).
Video Sharing: Platforms for video content (e.g., YouTube).
Messaging Platforms: Apps for text, voice, and video communication (e.g., WhatsApp).
Professional Networking: Connecting professionals for career development (e.g., LinkedIn).
Activism: Actions to promote social or political change.
Advocacy: Supporting or promoting a cause or policy.
Digital Literacy: Skills to effectively navigate digital information.
Information Overload: Difficulty in managing excessive information.

Exercise

Exercise 1 – Multiple Choice Questions

1. What was the first recognizable social media platform?
   A) Facebook
   B) Twitter
   C) Six Degrees
   D) MySpace

2. Which platform is known for professional networking?
   A) Instagram
   B) Twitter
   C) LinkedIn
   D) TikTok

3. Which year was Facebook launched?
   A) 2003
   B) 2004
   C) 2005
   D) 2006

4. What is Twitter primarily used for?
   A) Video sharing
   B) Microblogging
   C) Professional networking
   D) Photo sharing

5. Which platform focuses on short-form video content and gained popularity for viral challenges?
   A) Instagram
   B) Snapchat
   C) TikTok
   D) YouTube

Exercise 2 – True/False

1. Instagram focuses on text-based updates.

2. LinkedIn is a professional networking site.

3. YouTube was founded in 2010.

4. Facebook's News Feed was a significant innovation in social media.

5. TikTok is primarily used for sharing long-form video content.

Exercise 3 – Fill in the blanks

1. Social media platforms like Facebook and Twitter are known for ______ interactions.

2. The first recognizable social media platform was ______.

3. Instagram focuses primarily on ______ content sharing.

4. Twitter's messages are called ______.

5. LinkedIn is a platform designed for ______ networking.

Exercise 4- Small Answers

1. What is the primary function of Facebook?

2. How does Twitter facilitate real-time communication?

3. What distinguishes LinkedIn from other social media platforms?

4. What makes TikTok popular among younger audiences?

5. Explain the significance of the News Feed feature on Facebook.

Exercise 5- Long Answers

1. Discuss the evolution of social media from its early beginnings to the present day, highlighting key platforms and their impact on society.

2. Explain the multifaceted impact of social media on modern communication, providing examples from different aspects such as personal connections, business marketing, and political discourse.

Answer

Exercise 1- 1) C , 2) C , 3) B , 4) B , 5) C
Exercise 2- 1) False , 2) True , 3) False , 4) True , 5) False
Exercise 3- 1) real-time , 2) Six Degrees , 3) visual , 4) tweets , 5) professional
Exercise 4- 1) Facebook is primarily used for social networking, allowing users to connect with friends and family, share updates, photos, and videos.

2)Twitter allows users to post short text updates called tweets, which can be shared and viewed in real-time, making it a hub for real-time news updates and discussions.

3)LinkedIn is specifically designed for professional networking, enabling users to connect with colleagues, search for jobs, and participate in industry-related discussions.

4)TikTok's popularity among younger audiences is due to its focus on short-form video content, viral challenges, and creative expression through music and effects.

5)The News Feed feature on Facebook displays a curated stream of content from friends and pages users follow, keeping them updated on personal and public activities.

Chapter-11
TEST PAPER
Introduction to Computers

Time Duration: 30 Minutes **Maximum Marks: 25**

General Instructions:

1. The question paper consists of questions and is divided into four sections, A, B and C.
2. All questions are compulsory.
3. Section A comprises Fill in the blanks and one word of one mark each.
4. Section B comprises question numbers 1 to 5. These are Short Question carrying two marks each.
5. Section C comprises question numbers 1. These are Long Question carrying five marks each.

SECTION-A

Fill in the blanks- (1 X 5 = 5 marks)

1. The first recognizable social media platform was ______.
2. Facebook's feature that displays a curated stream of content from friends and pages is called the ______.
3. ______ is a social media platform known for its real-time news updates and discussions.
4. The video-sharing platform launched in 2005 is ______.
5. The platform that combines messaging and social networking features and was launched in China is ______.

One word- (1 X 5 = 5 marks)

1. What is the term for short text updates on Twitter?
2. Which social media platform is primarily used for professional networking?
3. What type of content is Instagram primarily known for?
4. Who is the creator of Facebook?
5. Which platform is famous for short-form videos and viral challenges?

SECTION-B

Short Question- (2 X 5 = 10 marks)

1. Explain the significance of LinkedIn for professional networking.
2. Discuss how Instagram supports personal expression through visual storytelling.
3. How has TikTok influenced content creation and consumption among younger audiences?
4. Describe the role of social media in facilitating global connectivity and collaboration.
5. What are the challenges associated with misinformation and disinformation on social media, and how can they be addressed?

SECTION-C

Long Question- . (5 marks)

1. Evaluate the impact of social media on modern communication, focusing on both positive and negative aspects. Provide examples from personal connections, business marketing, and political discourse.

ONLINE RESOURCES

Chapter 11 Practice Paper
Link
https://forms.gle/q9QtbNykSaK44U5UA
QR Code

Chapter 11 Video Content
Link
https://youtu.be/OYH6R6tByOU?si=x7M5etgypmzB2zdk
QR Code

Chapter 12: Artificial Intelligence

In this chapter you will learn about :

Basics of Artificial Intelligence (AI)

Historical perspective of AI

Applications of AI

In today's world, technology is growing very fast, and we are getting in touch with different new technologies day by day.
Here, one of the booming technologies of computer science is Artificial Intelligence which is ready to create a new revolution in the world by making intelligent machines. The Artificial Intelligence is now all around us. It is currently working with a variety of subfields, ranging from general to specific, such as self-driving cars, playing chess, proving theorems, playing music, Painting, etc.

12.1 Basics of Artificial Intelligence (AI)

Broadly speaking, Artificially Intelligent systems can perform tasks commonly associated with human cognitive functions — such as interpreting speech, playing games and identifying patterns. They typically learn how to do so by processing massive amounts of data, looking for patterns to model in their own decision-making. In many cases, humans will supervise an AI's learning process, reinforcing good decisions and discouraging bad ones. But some AI systems are designed to learn without supervision — for instance, by playing a video game over and over until they eventually figure out the rules and how to win.
Artificial Intelligence is the simulation of human intelligence processes by machines, especially computer systems. Specific applications of AI include Expert Systems,NnaturalLlanguage Processing, Speech Recognition and Machine Vision. Hear the term artificial intelligence (AI), you might think of self-driving cars, robots, ChatGPT or other AI chatbots, and artificially created images. But it's also important to look behind the outputs of AI and understand how the technology works and its impacts for none and future generations. AI is a concept that has been around, formally since the 1950s, when it was defined as a machine's ability to perform a task that would've previously required human intelligence. This is quite a broad definition and one that has been modified over decades of research and technological advancements. Artificial Intelligence (AI) is a wide-ranging branch of computer science concerned with building smart machines capable of performing tasks that typically require human intelligence. While AI is an interdisciplinary science with multiple approaches, advancements in machine learning and deep learning, in particular, are creating a paradigm shift in virtually every sector of the tech industry. Artificial Intelligence allows machines to model, or even improve upon, the capabilities of the human mind. And from the development of self-driving cars to the proliferation of generative AI tools like ChatGPT and Google's Bard, AI is increasingly becoming part of everyday life — and an area companies across every industry are investing in.
In Artificial Intelligence (AI), the term "agent" refers to an entity that perceives its environment through sensors and acts upon that environment through actuators to achieve specific goals. An AI agent can be anything that can be viewed as perceiving its environment through sensors and acting upon that environment through effectors.
Classification of AI Agents
AI agents can be classified based on their complexity and capabilities into several categories:

Simple Reflex Agents:
These agents select actions based on the current percept, ignoring the rest of the percept history.
They operate using condition-action rules, where specific conditions trigger specific actions.
Example: A thermostat that turns the heating on if the temperature drops below a certain point.

Model-Based Reflex Agents:
These agents maintain an internal state that depends on the percept history, which helps them handle partially observable environments.
They have a model of the world and use it to choose actions based on the current percept and the history of previous percepts.
Example: A robot vacuum cleaner that maps the layout of a room as it cleans.

Goal-Based Agents:
These agents act to achieve specific goals. They are designed to plan actions by considering future events and the desired goal state.
They use search and planning algorithms to find the sequence of actions that will achieve their goals.
Example: A chess-playing program that plans moves to checkmate the opponent.

Utility-Based Agents:
These agents maximize a utility function to make decisions that lead to the highest overall benefit.
They not only consider the goal but also evaluate the desirability of different outcomes.
Example: An autonomous car that considers multiple factors (safety, speed, fuel efficiency) to determine the best driving strategy.

Learning Agents:
These agents have the capability to learn from their experiences and improve their performance over time.
They include components such as learning elements, performance elements, and critic and problem generator.
Example: A recommendation system that improves its suggestions based on user feedback and behavior.

Multi-Agent Systems:
These systems involve multiple agents that interact with each other to achieve individual or collective goals.
Agents can be cooperative, competitive, or both, depending on the nature of the problem.
Example: A team of robots working together to carry out a search-and-rescue mission.

1.1.1 Strong AI Vs. Weak AI

Intelligence is tricky to define, which is why AI experts typically distinguish between strong AI and weak AI.

Strong AI - Strong AI, also known as Artificial General Intelligence, is a machine that can solve problems it's never been trained to work on — much like a human can. This is the kind of AI we see in movies, like the robots from Westworld or the character Data from Star Trek: The Next Generation. This type of AI doesn't actually exist yet. The creation of a machine with human-level intelligence that can be applied to any task is the Holy Grail for many AI researchers, but the quest for artificial general intelligence has been fraught with difficulty. And some believe strong AI research should be limited, due to the potential risks of creating a powerful AI without appropriate guardrails. In contrast to weak AI, strong AI represents a machine with a full set of cognitive abilities — and an equally wide array of use cases — but time hasn't eased the difficulty of achieving such a feat.

Weak AI - Weak AI, sometimes referred to as narrow AI or specialized AI, operates within a limited context and is a simulation of human intelligence applied to a narrowly defined problem (like driving a car, transcribing human speech or curating content on a website). Weak AI is often focused on performing a single task extremely well. While these machines may seem intelligent, they operate under far more constraints and limitations, than even the most basic human intelligence. Weak AI examples include:
Siri
Alexa and other smart assistants
Self-driving cars
Google search
Conversational bots
Email spam filters
Netflix's recommendations

12.1.2 TYPES OF ARTIFICIAL INTELLIGENCE
The Four Types of AI
AI can be divided into four categories, based on the type and complexity of the tasks a system is able to perform. They are:
1. Reactive machines
2. Limited memory
3. Theory of mind
4. Self awareness

1. Reactive Machines - A Reactive Machine follows the most basic of AI principles and, as its name implies, is capable of only using its intelligence to perceive and react to the world in front of it. A reactive machine cannot

store a memory and, as a result, cannot rely on past experiences to inform decision making in real time. Perceiving the world directly means that reactive machines are designed to complete only a limited number of specialized duties. Intentionally narrowing a reactive machine's worldview has its benefits, however: This type of AI will be more trustworthy and reliable, and it will react the same way to the same stimuli every time.

Reactive Machine Examples - Deep Blue was designed by IBM in the 1990s as a chess-playing supercomputer and defeated international grandmaster Gary Kasparov in a game. Deep Blue was only capable of identifying the pieces on a chess board and knowing how each moves based on the rules of chess, acknowledging each piece's present position and determining what the most logical move would be at that moment. The computer was not pursuing future potential moves by its opponent or trying to put its own pieces in better position. Every turn was viewed as its own reality, separate from any other movement that was made beforehand. Google's AlphaGo is also incapable of evaluating future moves but relies on its own neural network to evaluate developments of the present game, giving it an edge over Deep Blue in a more complex game. AlphaGo also bested world-class competitors of the game, defeating champion Go player Lee Sedol in 2016.

2. Limited Memory - Limited Memory AI has the ability to store previous data and predictions, when gathering information and weighing potential decisions — essentially looking into the past for clues on what may come next. Limited memory AI is more complex and presents greater possibilities than reactive machines. Limited memory AI is created when a team continuously trains a model in how to analyze and utilize new data, or an AI environment is built so models can be automatically trained and renewed. When utilizing limited memory AI in ML, six steps must be followed:

1. Establish training data
2. Create the machine learning model
3. Ensure the model can make predictions
4. Ensure the model can receive human or environmental feedback
5. Store human and environmental feedback as data
6. Reiterate the steps above as a cycle

3. Theory of Mind - Theory of mind is just that — theoretical. We have not yet achieved the technological and scientific capabilities necessary to reach this next level of AI. The concept is based on the psychological premise of understanding that other living things have thoughts and emotions that affect the behavior of one's self. In terms of AI machines, this would mean that AI could comprehend how humans, animals and other machines feel and make decisions through self-
reflection and determination, and then utilize that information to make decisions of their own. Essentially, machines would have to be able to grasp and process the concept of "mind," the fluctuations of emotions in decision-making and a litany of other psychological concepts in real time, creating a two-way relationship between people and AI.

4. Self Awareness - Once theory of mind can be established, sometime well into the future of AI, the final step will be for AI to become self-aware. This kind of AI possesses human-level consciousness and understands its own existence in the world, as well as the presence and emotional state of others. It would be able to understand what others may need based on not just what they communicate to them, but how they communicate it. Self-awareness in AI relies both on human researchers understanding the premise of consciousness and then learning how to replicate that, so it can be built into machines.

12.1.3 Artificial Intelligence Examples

Artificial intelligence technology takes many forms, from chatbots to navigation apps and wearable fitness trackers. The below examples illustrate the breadth of potential AI applications.

1. ChatGPT - ChatGPT is an artificial intelligence chatbot capable of producing written content in a range of formats, from essays to code and answers to simple questions. Launched in November 2022 by OpenAI, ChatGPT is powered by a large language model that allows it to closely emulate human writing.
2. Google Maps - Google Maps uses location data from smartphones, as well as user-reported data on things like construction and car accidents, to monitor the ebb and flow of traffic and assess what will be the fastest route.
3. Smart Assistants - Personal assistants like Siri, Alexa and Cortana use natural language processing, or NLP, to receive instructions from users to set reminders, search for online information and control the lights in people's homes. In many cases, these assistants are designed to learn a user's preferences and improve their experience over time with better suggestions and more tailored responses.
4. Snapchat Filters - Snapchat filters use ML algorithms to distinguish between an image's subject and the background, track facial movements and adjust the image on the screen based on what the user is doing.

5. Self-Driving Cars - Self-driving cars are a recognizable example of deep learning, since they use deep neural networks to detect objects around them, determine their distance from other cars, identify traffic signals and much more.
6. Wearables - The wearable sensors and devices used in the healthcare industry also apply deep learning to assess the health condition of the patient, including their blood sugar levels, blood pressure and heart rate. They can also derive patterns from a patient's prior medical data and use that to anticipate any future health conditions.
7. MuZero - MuZero, a computer program created by DeepMind, is a promising frontrunner in the quest to achieve true artificial general intelligence. It has managed to master games that has not even been taught to play, including chess and an entire suite of Atari games, through brute force, playing games millions of times.

12.2 Historical perspective of AI

The Foundations of Artificial Intelligence is a research area within Georgia Tech's School of Computer Science (SCS) that focuses on the development of algorithms, that leverage data and statistical tools to solve complex human tasks, to explore novel applications of such tools, and to better understand the apparent success of AI in practice. Instead of focusing on specific applications (e.g., Computer Vision, NLP or Robotics), the Foundations of Artificial Intelligence area focuses on general principles and novel approaches, that can be applied across a wide spectrum of applications. We are particularly interested in topics such as machine learning theory, scalable and distributed training, heterogeneity-aware inference, and robust dynamically adaptive algorithms, that help navigate multi-dimensional tradeoff spaces spanned by ML accuracy, model size, latency, and spatio-temporal cost efficiency of both training and inference. The Foundations of Artificial Intelligence area at SCS has made significant contributions in:
1. Online learning
2. Reinforcement learning
3. Systems support for distributed ML frameworks
4. Resource management for distributed ML frameworks
5. Continual learning
6. Learning theory
7. Federated learning
8. Auto ML
9. Explainable ML
10. Systems support for heterogeneity-aware ML inference
11. Neural Architecture Search (NAS)
12. Neuro-inspired AI

Our major sources of funding are the National Science Foundation (NSF) and the Defense Advanced Research Projects Agency (DARPA). Additionally, we participate in interdisciplinary research that brings together machine learning,
neuroscience, biology, mathematics and statistics, and theoretical computer science. We welcome the involvement of graduate and undergraduate students in our research projects and the broader intellectual community.

12.3 Applications of AI

AI has many uses — from boosting vaccine development to automating detection of potential fraud. AI companies raised $66.8 billion in funding in 2022, according to CB Insights research, more than double the amount raised in 2020. Because of its fast-paced adoption, AI is making waves in a variety of industries.
1. Safer Banking - Business Insider Intelligence's 2022 report on AI in banking found more than half of financial services companies already use AI solutions for risk management and revenue generation. The application of AI in banking could lead to upwards of $400 billion in savings.
2. Better Medicine - As for medicine, a 2021 World Health Organization report noted that while integrating AI into the healthcare field comes with challenges, the technology "holds great promise," as it could lead to benefits like more informed health policy and improvements in the accuracy of diagnosing patients.
3. Innovative Media - AI has also made its mark on entertainment. The global market for AI in media and entertainment is estimated to reach $99.48 billion by 2030, growing from a value of $10.87 billion in 2021, according to Grand View Research. That expansion includes AI uses, like recognizing plagiarism and developing high-definition graphics.

12.3.1 Future of Artificial Intelligence

When one considers the computational costs and the technical data infrastructure running behind artificial intelligence, actually executing on AI is a complex and costly business. Fortunately, there have been massive advancements in computing technology, as indicated by Moore's Law, which states that the number of transistors on a microchip doubles about every two years while the cost of computers is halved. Although many experts believe that Moore's Law will likely come to an end sometime in the 2020s, this has had a major impact on modern AI techniques — without it, deep learning would be out of the question, financially speaking. Recent research found that AI innovation has actually outperformed Moore's Law, doubling every six months or so, as opposed to two years. By that logic, the advancements artificial intelligence made across a variety of industries have been major over the last several years. And the potential for an even greater impact over the next several decades seems all but inevitable.

The future of AI is exciting, with many possibilities for innovation and development. Some of the future prospects of AI include:

1. Healthcare & Education - AI has the potential to revolutionize healthcare by enabling personalized treatment plans, improving diagnosis accuracy, and accelerating drug discovery. But there's more: It can also improve the education system by providing personalized learning experiences, automating administrative tasks, and facilitating remote learning. At Maker Faire Rome several projects have strongly demonstrated, over the years, how AI is an increasingly effective tool for predicting serious diseases such as diabetes mellitus. In 2021, a Machine Learning project, developed by Giacomo Bornino, Marco Chierici, Venet Osmani, Antonio Colangelo, Giuseppe Jurman, has shown how AI technologies are really able to predict five comorbidities from 17,000 blood tests and 23 variables, none of which were currently used as diagnostic criteria. The results have been promising to facilitate the early diagnosis of complications of diabetes mellitus, one of the leading causes of death worldwide. At Maker Faire Rome 2021 has been shown how AI can be use to predict Diabetes Mellitus.
2. Environment - AI can contribute to environmental sustainability by optimizing resource management, predicting natural disasters, and reducing carbon emissions.

12.3.2 Recent advancements in AI

AI has made significant strides in recent years, thanks to the development of advanced machine learning algorithms, deep learning techniques, and neural networks. Some of the recent advancements in AI include:

1. Natural Language Processing (NLP) - NLP is a subfield of AI that deals with the interaction between computers and human language. Recent advancements in NLP have led to the development of chatbots, virtual assistants, and voice recognition software, which have made communication between humans and machines more natural and seamless. An extremely interesting application of strong Artificial Intelligence has been proposed by a research group from the University of Bologna, which used a Deep Learning system for the first time to try to decipher a 3,500-year-old language: Minoan Cyprus. This language, widespread on the island of Cyprus in the Late Bronze Age, defied translators who tried to interpret it for more than a century, colliding with the lack of texts (just over two hundred) and the lack of bilingual works. Until today, in fact, scholars have not yet found a common ground on the number of characters in the alphabet of this language. Researchers therefore used unsupervised learning techniques, in which the model develops hypotheses and conclusions without previous knowledge of the language and signs to be analyzed. This gave birth to a real ad hoc model, called "Sign2Vecd", trained to analyze and catalog not only the different signs of Minoan Cyprus, but also entire sequences of signs. The results outlined a vector representation for each sign that can be viewed in three dimensions, offering scholars the ability to identify any errors in the transcription of the signs.

2. Computer Vision & Robotics - Computer vision is a field of AI that deals with the ability of computers to interpret and understand visual information from the world around us. Recent advancements in computer vision have led to the development of facial recognition technology, object detection, and self-driving cars, among others. Speaking about Robotics, It is the field of AI that deals with the design, construction, and operation of robots. Recent advancements in robotics have led to the development of intelligent robots that can perform a wide range of tasks, from manufacturing to healthcare to space exploration. About the use of AI for facial recognition, a new tool, called GFP-GAN (Generative Facial Prior-Generative Adversarial Network), has been developed to "fix" old portraits damaged by time, so that nothing is lost over the years. The result can be generated quickly by merging two AI models capable of "filling" the image with realistic details. As you can well imagine, the result generated by the AI cannot be perfect and could involve a "slight change of identity", but reviewing old photos in new life can prove interesting; it could even help elderly and memory-impaired people recall memories they hold dear.

12.3.3 Challenges and Limitations of AI

While AI is certainly viewed as an important and quickly evolving asset, this emerging field comes with its share of downsides. The Pew Research Center surveyed 10,260 Americans in 2021 on their attitudes toward AI. The results found 45 percent of respondents are equally excited and concerned, and 37 percent are more concerned than excited. Additionally, more than 40 percent of respondents said they considered driverless cars to be bad for society. Yet the idea of using AI to identify the spread of false information on social media was more well received, with close to 40 percent of those surveyed labeling it a good idea. AI is a boon for improving productivity and efficiency, while at the same time reducing the potential for human error. But there are also some disadvantages, like development costs and the possibility for automated machines to replace human jobs. It's worth noting, however, that the artificial intelligence industry stands to create jobs, too — some of which have not even been invented yet.

Despite the remarkable advancements in AI, there are still significant challenges that need to be addressed. Some of the most pressing challenges facing AI include:
1) Data Bias - Data bias is a significant challenge in AI, as it can lead to algorithms that perpetuate discrimination and inequality. This is particularly problematic in areas such as facial recognition technology, where biased data can lead to inaccurate identification and unjust consequences.
2) Ethical Concerns & Human – AI Collaboration - AI raises several ethical concerns, such as privacy, autonomy, and accountability. For instance, the use of AI in decision-making processes, such as hiring or loan approvals, can lead to unfair outcomes if the algorithms are biased or flawed. As AI becomes more prevalent in various industries, it is essential to ensure that humans can collaborate with AI systems effectively. This requires developing user-friendly interfaces and designing AI systems that can explain their decisions and actions to humans. "Restorative AI" is able to fix old portraits and collect memories.

Summary

AI simulates human intelligence, performing tasks such as speech interpretation, game playing, and pattern recognition by processing large data sets.
Strong AI can solve new problems independently, while Weak AI operates within a limited context to perform specific tasks.
AI types include Reactive Machines, Limited Memory, Theory of Mind, and Self-awareness, each with increasing complexity and capability.
AI development has been marked by milestones in machine learning, neural networks, and distributed ML frameworks.
AI is used in banking, medicine, media, and various other industries to improve efficiency, accuracy, and innovation.
Future advancements in AI will likely impact healthcare, education, and environmental sustainability, among other fields.

Glossary

Deep Learning: A type of machine learning involving neural networks with multiple layers.
Natural Language Processing (NLP) : AI field focused on the interaction between computers and human language.
Reactive Machines : AI systems that respond to specific inputs without storing past experiences.

Limited Memory AI : AI systems that can use past experiences to inform current decision-making.
Neural Networks: Computing systems inspired by the human brain's network of neurons.
Federated Learning: Machine learning approach that trains algorithms across decentralized devices while keeping data local.
Data Bias : The presence of systematic error in data that leads to unfair outcomes in AI algorithms.
Ethical AI : The practice of designing and implementing AI systems in a way that adheres to ethical principles and guidelines.
Predictive Analytics : The use of AI to analyze data and make predictions about future events.

Previous Year Solved Question Paper

1. What do you understand by the term agent in AI ? Clasify them.[IGNOU MCA-2019]

ANS: In Artificial Intelligence (AI), the term "agent" refers to an entity that perceives its environment through sensors and acts upon that environment through actuators to achieve specific goals. An AI agent can be anything that can be viewed as perceiving its environment through sensors and acting upon that environment through effectors.

Classification of AI Agents

AI agents can be classified based on their complexity and capabilities into several categories:

Simple Reflex Agents:

These agents select actions based on the current percept, ignoring the rest of the percept history.

They operate using condition-action rules, where specific conditions trigger specific actions.

Example: A thermostat that turns the heating on if the temperature drops below a certain point.

Model-Based Reflex Agents:

These agents maintain an internal state that depends on the percept history, which helps them handle partially observable environments.

They have a model of the world and use it to choose actions based on the current percept and the history of previous percepts.

Example: A robot vacuum cleaner that maps the layout of a room as it cleans.

Goal-Based Agents:

These agents act to achieve specific goals. They are designed to plan actions by considering future events and the desired goal state.

They use search and planning algorithms to find the sequence of actions that will achieve their goals.

Example: A chess-playing program that plans moves to checkmate the opponent.

Utility-Based Agents:

These agents maximize a utility function to make decisions that lead to the highest overall benefit.
They not only consider the goal but also evaluate the desirability of different outcomes.
Example: An autonomous car that considers multiple factors (safety, speed, fuel efficiency) to determine the best driving strategy.

Learning Agents:

These agents have the capability to learn from their experiences and improve their performance over time.
They include components such as learning elements, performance elements, and critic and problem generator.
Example: A recommendation system that improves its suggestions based on user feedback and behavior.

Multi-Agent Systems:

These systems involve multiple agents that interact with each other to achieve individual or collective goals.
Agents can be cooperative, competitive, or both, depending on the nature of the problem.
Example: A team of robots working together to carry out a search-and-rescue mission.

Previous Year Unsolved Question Paper

1.What are the uncertainity of AI?[IGNOU MCA-2019]

Exercise

Exercise 1 – Multiple Choice Questions

1. Which type of AI can solve problems it has never been trained on?
   A) Reactive AI
   B) Weak AI
   C) Limited Memory AI
   D) Strong AI

2. What is the main characteristic of Reactive Machines in AI?
   A) Storing past experiences
   B) Understanding human emotions
   C) Responding to specific inputs without memory
   D) Performing multiple tasks simultaneously

3. Which AI application uses NLP to understand user commands?
   A) Self-driving cars
   B) Smart assistants
   C) Google Maps
   D) Deep Blue

4. Google's AlphaGo is an example of which type of AI?
   A) Reactive Machines
   B) Limited Memory AI
   C) Strong AI
   D) Self-awareness AI

5. Which subfield of AI deals with the interaction between computers and human language?
   A) Robotics
   B) NLP
   C) Deep Learning
   D) Computer Visio

Exercise 2 – True/False

Artificial Intelligence can perform tasks commonly associated with human cognitive functions.

Weak AI can solve problems it has never been trained to work on.

Limited Memory AI cannot use past data to make predictions.

Reactive machines can rely on past experiences to inform real-time decision-making.

Strong AI, also known as Artificial General Intelligence, currently exists and is widely used.

Exercise 3 – Fill in the blanks

1. Artificial Intelligence can be broadly divided into ______ AI and ______ AI.
2. ______ is a subfield of AI that deals with the interaction between computers and human language.
3. Limited Memory AI can store ______ data and use it to make predictions.
4. Reactive machines follow the most basic AI principles and cannot ______ past experiences.
5. The AI chatbot developed by OpenAI and capable of producing written content in a range of formats is known as ______.

Exercise 4- Small Answers

1. What is Artificial Intelligence (AI)?
2. What distinguishes Strong AI from Weak AI?
3. Name two examples of Weak AI.
4. What are Reactive Machines in AI?
5. What is Natural Language Processing (NLP)?

Exercise 5- Long Answers

1. Discuss the historical development of Artificial Intelligence (AI) and its key milestones.
2. Explain the different types of AI: Reactive Machines, Limited Memory, Theory of Mind, and Self-Awareness.

Answer

Exercise 1- 1) D , 2) C , 3) B , 4) A , 5) B

Exercise 2- 1) True , 2) False , 3) False , 4) False , 5) False

Exercise 3- 1) Weak, Strong , 2) NLP , 3) previous , 4) store, 5) ChatGPT

Exercise 4- 1) AI is the simulation of human intelligence processes by machines, especially computer systems, including learning, reasoning, and self-correction.

2)Strong AI can solve problems independently across a range of tasks, whereas Weak AI is designed for specific tasks within a limited context.

3)Siri and Google Search.

4)Reactive Machines are AI systems that respond to specific inputs without storing past experiences.

5)NLP is a subfield of AI focused on the interaction between computers and human language.

Chapter-12
TEST PAPER
Introduction to Computers

Time Duration: 30 Minutes **Maximum Marks: 25**

General Instructions:

1. The question paper consists of questions and is divided into four sections, A, B and C.
2. All questions are compulsory.
3. Section A comprises Fill in the blanks and one word of one mark each.
4. Section B comprises question numbers 1 to 5. These are Short Question carrying two marks each.
5. Section C comprises question numbers 1. These are Long Question carrying five marks each.

SECTION-A

Fill in the blanks- **(1 X 5 = 5 marks)**

1. _________ AI refers to AI systems that operate within a narrow context and perform specific tasks.
2. _________ learning involves algorithms that can improve themselves over time through experience without being explicitly programmed.
3. _________ is a subfield of AI that focuses on the interaction between computers and human language.
4. The AI model _________ was designed by OpenAI and is capable of generating human-like text based on given prompts.
5. In AI, _________ learning involves training models on a labeled dataset, where the correct output is known.

One word- **(1 X 5 = 5 marks)**

1. What is the term for AI systems that learn from and improve with data without human intervention?
2. What kind of AI is depicted by a machine capable of human-level cognition across diverse tasks?
3. What is the AI subfield that focuses on enabling machines to understand and respond to human language?
4. Which technology uses AI to generate realistic human-like text based on input prompts?
5. What term describes AI systems that have the ability to understand and interpret visual information from the world?

SECTION-B

Short Question- **(2 X 5 = 10 marks)**

1. What is the primary difference between reactive machines and limited memory AI?
2. How do self-driving cars utilize AI to ensure safe navigation?
3. Name two ethical concerns associated with the deployment of AI technologies.
4. What is the purpose of Federated Learning in AI?
5. Describe one application of AI in environmental sustainability.

SECTION-C

Long Question- . **(5 marks)**

1. Discuss the various types of AI, specifically focusing on Reactive Machines, Limited Memory, Theory of Mind, and Self-Awareness. Explain each type's capabilities, examples, and potential future advancements.

ONLINE RESOURCES

Chapter 12 Practice Paper
Link
https://forms.gle/hk2qYXXfVW1LoYit8
QR Code

Chapter 12 Video Content
Link
https://youtu.be/S28k48Wb8mI?si=PjORDPe3rpZjBPv0
QR Code

VIVA VOCE

1. What is a system in the context of system analysis and design?

Ans: A system is a group of interrelated components that work together to perform a specific task or achieve a common goal.

2. What are the key phases of the System Development Lifecycle (SDLC)?

Ans: The key phases are Analysis, Design, Development, Implementation, and Maintenance.

3. What role does a systems analyst play in system development?

Ans: A systems analyst investigates and understands user needs, gathers requirements, designs the system, and ensures it is built correctly.

4. Define 'systems thinking.'

Ans: Systems thinking is an approach to problem-solving that views complex entities as whole systems, considering the interconnections and interactions between components.

5. What is a use case diagram?

Ans: A use case diagram is a visual representation of the interactions between users (actors) and the system, showing the different ways the system will be used.

6. What is the purpose of an entity-relationship (ER) diagram?

Ans: An ER diagram is used to illustrate the relationships between entities within a database.

7. What is normalization in database design?

Ans: Normalization is the process of organizing data in a database to reduce redundancy and improve data integrity.

8. What is the difference between primary memory and secondary memory?

Ans: Primary memory (RAM) is volatile and used for temporary data storage while the system is running, whereas secondary memory (e.g., hard drives) is non-volatile and used for long-term storage.

9. What is the role of a project manager in system development?

Ans: A project manager plans the project, assigns tasks, monitors progress, manages the budget, and ensures the project stays on track.

10. What is Agile methodology?

Ans: Agile methodology is an iterative and incremental approach to software development that emphasizes flexibility, collaboration, and customer feedback.

11. What is a binary system?

Ans: The binary system is a number system that uses only two digits, 0 and 1, and is the basis for data representation in computers.

12. What are the core components of a computer system?

Ans: The core components are the CPU, memory (RAM), storage devices, input devices (e.g., keyboard), and output devices (e.g., monitor).

13. What is the function of the CPU?

Ans: The CPU (Central Processing Unit) executes instructions and performs calculations to process data.

14. What is an operating system (OS)?

Ans: An OS is system software that manages computer hardware and provides services for application software.

15. What are some common types of input devices?

Ans: Common input devices include keyboards, mice, touchscreens, and microphones.

16. Define 'algorithm.'

Ans: An algorithm is a step-by-step procedure or set of instructions for solving a problem or performing a specific task.

17. What is the role of a database management system (DBMS)?

Ans: A DBMS manages data storage, retrieval, and manipulation in a database.

18. What is the purpose of a data flow diagram (DFD)?

Ans: A DFD visually represents the flow of data within a system, showing how data is processed by the system's components.

19. What is cloud computing?

Ans: Cloud computing is the delivery of computing services, such as storage and processing power, over the internet.

20. What is a relational database?

Ans: A relational database is a database structured to recognize relationships among stored data using tables.

ONLINE RESOURCES

Viva Voce Video

Link

https://youtu.be/HC7CXaPI_bc?si=R8c0Xk39V183F5hv

QR Code

Computer Fundamentals Annual Exam Papers

Sample Paper - 1

Time Duration: 2 Hours Maximum Marks: 50

General Instructions:

1. Answer any 20 questions out of the given 24 questions of 1 mark each.
2. Answer any 10 questions from the given 12 questions of 2 marks each.
3. Answer any 2 questions from the given 4 questions of 5 marks each.
4. This question paper contains 40 questions out of which 32 questions are to be answered.
5. All questions of a particular part/section must be attempted in the correct order.
6. The maximum time allowed is 2 hrs

SECTION A

1. What does EPROM stand for?

a. Electrically Programmable Read-Only Memory

b. Erasable Programmable Read-Only Memory

c. Encoded Programmable ROM

d. Extended PROM

2. What is the maximum storage capacity of a standard single-layer DVD?

a. 700 MB

b. 1.44 MB

c. 4.7 GB

d. 128 GB

3. What does GUI stand for in the context of operating systems?

a. General Utility Interface

b. Graphical User Interface

c. General User Input

d. Graphical Utility Input

4. Which type of software is designed to help produce documents and presentations?

a. Media software

b. Utility programs

c. Productivity software

d. System software

5. The Unicode standard uses how many bits to represent characters?

a. 7 bits

b. 8 bits

c. Multiple bytes

d. 16 bits

6. What does ASCII stand for?

a. American Standard Code for Information Interchange

b. American Secure Code for Internet Interchange

c. Automated Standard Code for Information Interchange

d. Advanced System Code for Information Interchange

7. What type of network is the internet considered to be?

a. LAN

b. WAN

c. MAN

d. PAN

8. Which protocol is used for sending web pages over the internet?

a. TCP

b. FTP

c. HTTP

d. SMTP

9. Which security measure involves using two different authentication factors?

a. Single Sign-On

b. Two-Factor Authentication

c. Password Management

d. Biometric Authentication

10. Which of the following is an ethical issue in computing?

a. Data encryption

b. Privacy concerns

c. System updates

d. Network topology

11. What is the primary function of the Control Unit in the Von Neumann architecture?

a. Perform arithmetic operations

b. Execute I/O operations

c. Fetch, decode, and execute instructions

d. Store data

12. Which of the following is NOT an advantage of high-level programming languages?

a. Ease of use

b. Portability

c. Detailed hardware control

d. Faster development

13. In the C programming language, what does the `#include <stdio.h>` statement do?

a. Includes the standard input/output library

b. Starts the main function

c. Declares a variable

d. Ends the program

14. Which looping statement in Python is used to iterate over a sequence of elements?

a. while

b. for

c. do-while

d. until

5. The division operation in relational algebra is used to:

a. Retrieve records from one table related to all records in another table

b. Combine rows from two tables

c. Select specific columns

d. Filter rows based on a condition

6. What is the purpose of the UPDATE statement in SQL?

a. To retrieve data

b. To add new records

c. To modify existing records

d. To delete records

7. What is the main advantage of using Microsoft Access?

a. Creating presentations

b. Managing large datasets

c. Email communication

d. Word processing

8. In PowerPoint, what is the purpose of the Slide Master?

a. To add animations

b. To control the overall design and layout

c. To create tables

d. To edit text

9. What is a primary ethical concern with AI?

a. Efficiency

b. Data Privacy

c. Speed

d. Usability

10. Which type of AI operates within a limited context and performs specific tasks?

a. Strong AI

b. Reactive Machines

c. Weak AI

d. Self-awareness AI

SECTION B

1. What is a mainframe computer used for?
2. What does EPROM stand for and how can it be modified?
3. What is the significance of programming languages in computing?
4. Explain the conversion process from binary to octal.
5. Define latency in the context of data communication.
6. What distinguishes a Metropolitan Area Network (MAN) from a WAN?
7. What are the ethical concerns related to data privacy in computing?
8. Give an example of a high-profile hacking incident and its impact.
9. What are the advantages of using high-level programming languages?
10. Explain the concept of pipelining in the context of Instruction Set Architecture (ISA).
11. What is functional programming and how does it differ from procedural programming?
12. What is a composite key and when is it used?

SECTION C

1. Discuss how input and output devices enhance the functionality of computers.
2. Explain how educational software enhances learning and provide examples of how it is used.
3. Discuss the significance of ASCII and Unicode in data representation.
4. Examine the ethical and legal considerations of data privacy in the context of modern technology.
5. Computer Fundamentals Annual Exam Papers

YouTube Videos Playlists for all Chapters

CHAPTER 1
Link
https://www.youtube.com/playlist?list=PLzlh_31VWEFpGs-g6eWSPm6CsA018uRcy

CHAPTER 2
Link
https://www.youtube.com/playlist?list=PLzlh_31VWEFqI4Wonucrh6Dslm1YirsLo
QR Code

CHAPTER 3
Link
https://www.youtube.com/playlist?list=PLzlh_31VWEFpjEVisU5V0KuxAM8RfOM9u
QR Code

CHAPTER 4
Link
https://www.youtube.com/playlist?list=PLzlh_31VWEFruOq6KBh8x2-CcFYWGSq2n
QR Code

CHAPTER 5
Link
https://www.youtube.com/playlist?list=PLzlh_31VWEFqVAcrQ3I9w5RJO7omQSl4A
QR Code

CHAPTER 6
Link
https://www.youtube.com/playlist?list=PLzlh_31VWEFr7mBvjm7LKdLYum_6GGBNa
QR Code

CHAPTER 7
Link
https://www.youtube.com/playlist?list=PLzlh_31VWEFoJPD68Eb4H0V2j4OOKzuZG
QR Code

CHAPTER 8
Link
https://www.youtube.com/playlist?list=PLzlh_31VWEFrdXlukNKDgBjnhiDIuWVMA
QR Code

CHAPTER 9
Link
https://www.youtube.com/playlist?list=PLzlh_31VWEFpqd_WEWxLhLtVeJcapgAX6
QR Code

CHAPTER 10
Link
https://www.youtube.com/playlist?list=PLzlh_31VWEFojw_BELcF2tQV18fOwfJiH
QR Code

CHAPTER 11
Link
https://www.youtube.com/playlist?list=PLzlh_31VWEFo1xerecjGi2vDi_Fl3FAFE

QR Code

CHAPTER 12

Link

https://www.youtube.com/playlist?list=PLzlh_31VWEFpkbpu8cLC6nZ9jy6x2Ovbx

QR Code